BLACKMAN: TOO HARD FOR YOU

Blackman: Too Hard For You

Samson Kamara (Sr.)

iUniverse, Inc.

New York Bloomington Shanghai

Blackman: Too Hard For You

iUniverse books may be ordered through booksellers or by contacting:

iUniverse
1663 Liberty Drive
Bloomington, IN 47403
www.iuniverse.com
1-800-Authors (1-800-288-4677)

Because of the dynamic nature of the Internet, any Web addresses or links contained in this book may have changed since publication and may no longer be valid.

The views expressed in this work are solely those of the author and do not necessarily reflect the views of the publisher, and the publisher hereby disclaims any responsibility for them.

ISBN: 978-0-595-48486-7 (pbk)
ISBN: 978-0-595-60578-1 (ebk)

Printed in the United States of America

Contents

The experiences of a Black African student at the University of Birmingham

CHAPTER 1

▼

It was a nice evening not too cold. Eddie arrived with some anxiety, not knowing what he was going to get out of the first evening at the University. He had mixed feeling about the place and the lecturers after the first encounter some months back. He looked at the tall building and round the campus with the imposing tower building on the other side of the campus. He went through the two double glass doors into the foyer. He went into the lift to the fifth floor. The door to the hall was open and he could see the black folks he lived with at the international house. He walked in. The hall was full of anxious faces from around the world. There was a long table full of men and women all well dressed. Those must be the guys who teach in the school of education. They must be the folks who would determine our fate in here, he thought. He was ushered to a seat at the back of the rest of the student body. Eddie looked round the packed hall. There were more black people of African descent all in suites. Some old, some quite young and ladies all simply dressed. The speaker it seemed to Eddie was the man who occupied the central position, with a different arm chair. The fellows sitting round him must be his staff. This could not be a school for African people he told himself. There was no black person there and not even a colored person. They were all English. How could all white people teach all black students? It was not fair, wasn't it?.

Every one was taken by surprise as the Professor knock on the desk for attention. "May I have your attention please, an elderly voice of the man with white beard, of medium build, about five feet six inches tall, with a gray suit and bright red tie?

He moved towards the center of the hall. He walked slowly with his head slightly towards his right shoulder. May I have your attention please he repeated.

This time the hall went dead silent except Talean's immaculate steps as she tip toed back to her seat.

He stood silent, folded his arms across his chest. He looked round and ended at Talean, as she lowered herself in the seat. The front desk with all those well dressed guys all sat silent and looked at the Professor.

"Right" he said. "The purpose of this gathering was to welcome you all into the University and the school of education. It was also to give you some back ground information and to clarify some points. We would like your start with us to be as comfortable as possible.

Eddie was not listening to the Professor's opening speech. He was looking straight at the Professor, but through him into the land of Utopia, day dreaming of course. He was thinking about the lady by his side, how to make a good impression of himself. He had not had a girlfriend for nearly a year now. "I think I could be sailing to the Cape of Good Hope" he told himself. But I have to get it right here and now.

The man was making faces at her now and again. I must not let him over took me for sure" he told himself.

Talean looked round. "You alright?" she said to Eddie with a smile in a soft voice.

"Ya man, I am alright, he replied in a strong manly voice.

"You were not listening to what the Professor was saying though" she went on. "Your eyes were all over the place. You were day dreaming weren't you? She cautioned.

"No. man, I was listening of course. But I was thinking about what I am going to do this evening.

I was also thing about you as well." he told her in a calm voice.

"What about tonight? You worried about something?" she asked in a curious voice.

He shifted and sat back in his seat. "No, not at all, as far as the academic work was concerned" he replied in a confident voice. "I did not think it was going to be that challenging. I am used to it now." He told her with confidence. "I was at Leeds University last year, you know."

She looked with curious eyes. "Doing what? "She asked with a curious voice and anxiety.

"A diploma in school administration." he replied.

"Well, look Eddie" She touch his shoulder hesitatingly. "I look alright up here, but deep, deep down, everything was tumbling and bubbling .I have not been to a University before. I did do a diploma from London, but I am not sure it prepared me enough to do a masters degree. I wanted to do just a certificate which I hoped to do with confident. But I felt some emptiness in my head and Tommy.

I did not hope that I would live up to the expectations of the course. That worried me a lot. You get what I mean?" She pulled herself round to face Eddie and moved closer to him. Her left thigh touched Eddie's right leg "I have no confidence in my self, you know. I am worried about a lot of things." She was pouring her feelings about her self and the course to Eddie.

As Talean transferred some of her weight to Eddie's right leg, he felt like an electric current flowing from her to him. He was taking in the weight like a child seeping in a sweet drink Elated and happy inside him, he listened like a marooned person receiving a radio message. He was taking in every word, he responded with body language, nodding now and again. He now and again looked straight into her eyes, smiled and showed keen interest in her conversation.

The Professor's address was going on, but Eddie was involved in a more interesting and absorbing side conversation in a low voice which only the two of them could hear.

"That was not a good start" he told her. "You should be confident of your self right at the start and then you go on building on that confidence as you got along. If you were not confident now, you were going to get less and less confident as time went by and the work would pile up. You should be able to generate more energy on the way. Things do get a lot tougher as you got on with the course. But the most important thing was faith and self confident in your ability to carry on to the end."

She put her hand over her mouth, paused for a second. "That was true, but my worry was that I am on a full time job in Handsworth. Doing a full time job and a full time Masters course I felt was a bit too much for me and may be too ambitious. You see what I mean? Besides that the Professor had told me that the course was very difficult." She indicated that right at the start.

Eddie looked at Talean straight in the face. "Look here, do not listen to what these people tell you, they try to frighten you off the course. They felt that because you are black, you have an inferior brain. I was told at the interview by the man sitting in that corner with the gray suit and white tie and long beard that the course was for white only.

He told me that he did not think I will be able to do it. It was too difficult for me. You see that lady sitting in the middle of the first row, with the pink dress on, and holding the orange drink."

"Oh yes," she replied. She is Mrs. Bolton; I met her in the library the other day. I have spoken to her, and she seemed alright to me" she said softly.

"Do you want to know what I told them at the interview?"

"No' she replied, looking with wide open eyes and holding her breath

"I told them that if any one had done this course before and graduated successfully, I would do it and graduate as well.

"Oh no," she pot her hand over her mouth. "You see you are a man, you are stronger; you can afford to speak your mind, because you are confident of yourself. I am a woman I am not confident of myself, and I would not be able to speak like that, you get what I mean?" she said in a forced voice.

What they have told me has made me even less confident of myself. I am frightened of the fact that I might not make it at the end of the day which will be shameful." She shuffled her legs and moved closer.

Eddie knew that she was getting tuned up to him. "You know what, you get to be very bold sometimes and speak your mind and let people know that you have confident in yourself. I knew that what I was saying was true and I believed in my self and proud of my ability," he said emphatically to impress the lady who was now getting hooked up to his charm.

As the conversation got more and more intimate, he could feel Talean's weight on his right leg. He bent his right leg slightly to accommodate the weight. The leg got heavier and stinking sensation of pain was reaching his brain. But his mind told him to absorb the pain. "I want to be able to move this leg at the end of the evening" he told himself.

The conversation got more and more interesting. They were now talking tete a tete and had moved to an exclusive world of their own, Eddie now sat face to face with Talean. She had moved the third time so close to him that he could feel the heat moving from her body to his thigh. The hall now has students and lectures all talking in small pockets, socializing with the lecturers.

"You are very brave man" she told him. "That statement was very bold. I would not be that up front with any of these people, because I know that I would not be able to produce the goods in the end." She said laughing.

Eddie looked at her, he shook his head slightly. "Well, I meant what I said and I will live by my words.

I hope to remind him at the end of the course."

"You know that they look down on us because we are colored. But some of us are more clever than most of them. After all, they study one thing and call themselves experts. That tiny world of theirs is all that they protect and preserve. I tell you what, opportunity has been our handicap" he told her. We have not been exposed to all of these ideas they specialized in, otherwise most black people would be experts, because they have more experience in most things which a white man would tell you I have never heard of it. If we had the same opportunity like them, we would have done better than most of those who call themselves experts.

Talean put her right hand over her mouth, then under her chin. "I am still worried and undecided, because the work is demanding. It is going to be more demanding than I would be able to give. I am going to drop from the course sooner or later" she said in a low unsure voice.

Eddie looked at her. He could see lines of fright and doubts in her eyes. She looked really confused and uncertain what to do next.

He smiled and then lifted his head up." You could not think of quitting the course when you have not even started yet. You need to start and see how far you could go with it before you make a decision. By quitting right away, you are confirming what these white folks think about us the black people, that we are inferior and not up to anything. I am not going to let you reinforce these peoples' feelings about us. I would not let you do that. No, no way. You are not going to drop off from the course, not at this time anyway, and not when I am doing the same course with you.

She listened to Eddie like a bull work who does all the ground work, advice and feed on the facts as presented to him.

She looked at Eddie for a few seconds. She frowned her face, tightened her mouth. "But if I can't, I can't cope. Simple as that" she said with a sharp tone.

"Hold on" he told her. "As long as I am here, you are in safe pair of hands." He held out his hands up in the air, his mouth open, as if he was praying, and his eyes bulging out.

She looked at Eddie, brightened her eyes and a big smile. She exclaimed. "Oh, you are going to help me with the assignments? She clapped her hands on her thighs. She now looked elated. Confidence had returned into her mind. "Oh you are an angel. You are a God send person." She changed her position with excitement. I would be sitting next to you during lectures and pick your brains. I am still not too confident of myself, you know. I am not also confident of what I want to do. It's like trying it out and sees what it was like. I like trying things out and you by my side I should be able to do it and produce the required goods. The Professor told me that I might have to do it over two years."

Eddie looked at her with stern eyes. "Two years, why would you want to do it for two years? It was a one year course" he told her.

Eddie felted a bit elated, he pushed closer to Talean.

She was the only black woman in the hall. All eyes were on her now. Her bright colored blue dress, covering her knees, light blue high heels. Her head was freshly platted with tiny braids, falling round her head. She had dark sun glasses. Her purse was on her lap and her hand bag besides her. She seemed to catch the eyes of the audience when she got up and went out of the hall briefly.

I must be the lucky guy tonight Eddie told himself. This was my day. She was mine. I would not let any one chat her up, not when I am here and always around.

Eddie had a temporal relief of pain from his right thing. She came back and sat by him. She seemed to have been overcome by excitement, at the prospect of doing the course with the help of Eddie.

She put her two hands on her breast, then exclaimed" I am breathing a deep sigh of relief, you know. It was like drinking cold water on a very hot afternoon."

Talean put her hands on Eddie's head and said" I trust your words."

Suddenly she turned round and looked around the large hall full of students from various parts of the world and the whole Education faculty. She pulled herself, and pulled her hands from Eddie quickly. She put both hands over her mouth, looked round the room again. She realized that she was the only black woman. I hoped no one saw what had happened. She pulled herself away in disgust. She sat straight. She then realized that she was leaning on Eddie all the while. "Oh God" she exclaimed. "This was not right at all, honest. This is the first night and the first time we are meeting. It's in a public place with millions of eyes. All the Professors and fellow students were watching. What would all these people think about me? Who would they think I am? That was going too far. I was too excited about what you were saying" she said. "I lost control of my self. You appeared so friendly, assuring me that I did not know what I was doing. I got too close to you the very first time I met you. I hope I did not create a bad impression of myself to the lecturers, because they know that I am married. "Excuse me" she said abruptly she got up and rushed to the toilet.

CHAPTER 2

▼

Talean was standing in the corridor outside the hall. She was trying to fix her dress and her underwear.

A tall man in brown suit and a bow tie came close to her stopped in front of her. "You alright?" he asked. He introduced himself as Dr. Pete.

Dr Pete?" she asked.

"Well, I am a Doctor, but you could call me Pete. I didn't mind. That would do for the day. We were trying to create an atmosphere of equality and friendliness. You enjoy your first night so far?" he asked.

"Oh yes. I like it here. I feel relaxed and the atmosphere was very friendly. The students were very friendly and assuring." She smiled and melted as she spoke to the lecturer for the first time.

I could see you were having a good conversation with your colleague," he said quietly.

She looked at him, folded her hands across her breast, she got up and stood straight.

"Oh yes, we were talking about the course and where we came from. He was telling me about Africa, the different cultures and people which I never knew. I did not know that Africa was a big continent, with lots of countries and cultures and international boarders. As Talean got more excited about talking to him, Pete walked away saying "I hope you enjoy the rest of the course."

She went and sat near Eddie again. She did not look at him. She looked away at the lecturers, as they move out one after another.

"You alright?' he said to Talean.

"I am alright" she replied, looking a bit tense and her face had changed from the happy non stop smiling out look to one of meek and serious outlook. Her mouth was tightened up and drawn. Her facial muscles had been tightened up and small wrinkles ran across her face.

"What was the matter with you?" Eddie asked.

She shifted herself, put both hands on the seat besides her like supporting her body.

"Nothing really," she said in a cold and calm voice. "I felt ashamed of myself when I touch your head and wanted to give you a peck on your cheek. I thought that was going too far in a public place" she told him in a calm and quiet voice.

"Nonsense that was" he replied. "These people have nothing to do with your feelings and you have to be yourself. You did what was right for you and stand up for what you believe was alright" He showed some concern about her beliefs. He tried to talk to her and convince her that nothing was out of the ordinary.

"You did not have to feel inhibited to express your feelings, when ever and where ever you were. These people could not and should not dictate how you expressed yourself and how you should behave before them. They were just ordinary people and they were only here to teach us some things we need to know, and not how we should behave ordinarily. We have our own customs and culture different from theirs. They could not prescribe our behavior and what we should do before them. We are black and different from them. We should feel free to express ourselves."

"But not in this flipping place with a thousand eyes all around watching you. Besides I had not known you before. I let myself down. I was carried away by your offer of helping me through the course. Remember, I am a married woman. Not a call girl. I have to behave like a married woman" She opened her eyes wide, put her index finger up and forward to tell Eddie to keep himself off and to warn him to behave himself. She looked with guilty eyes and her body language was one of some one who had committed an unforgivable crime. "I let myself down in this place with all these people around. I looked foolish and not up to my standard as a married woman.

"Don't be silly" Eddie told her in an aggressive tone. "Who would ever think like that? They knew that we were both black and we have common problems. We have to stick together and stop this people from pulling us down. United we stand against the frustration, the disgusting treatment we received each and every day" Eddie looked round and then at Talean and then bent his head down like someone making silent prayers.

She looked at Eddie with a curious eye. "You are right, you know" she said.

"I got frustrated every day at work and when I got home, my relatives frustrate me as well. I have no one to talk to. I just locked myself up in my bedroom and sometime I got bored to the point of anticipating suicide."

Eddie lifted his head up and looked at her with screwed eyes.

"Suicide, flipping heck, why mention that word here? That idea should have never crossed your mind for God's shake. It was quite not African to mention suicide, because we were very strong constitutionally and could cope with any situation. A typical African would never commit suicide, because we always thought out solutions to any problem and some times came up with many options. Those who commit suicide were those who think there were no solutions to their problems and so suicide was the only solution. It was a white man's idea because they were weak in constitution, and shallow minded and have no second thought about any thing and to die they think was the solution to inherent problems.

She pulled her lips together, changed her position. "Yes" she replied in a sharp tone. "It had a few times and I have thought about it, honest. I got really bored at work and at home. My Aunt really got on my nerves in the evenings. I did get really, really bored, frustrated and lonesome a lot of the time. That was the time when lots of stupid things came into my mind. Sometimes I felt that there was no solution to my problems. I did get funny feelings you know, like been trapped in a situation and no way out of it, and the feeling of helplessness." She looked at Eddie, his face showed signs of disapproval.

Eddie had released the tension on his leg. He felt more relaxed now; and listened more attentively than ever.

Eddie straightened his back bone. "Look here Talean, you would never be bored again. This course was demanding and with your full time job as well. You would have more than enough to keep you busy all day and all the time. It's more than a plate full for you, believe it or not.

Talean looked a bit worried. She clenched her fists with some unease. She looked round as if she was testing the air. "I thought someone was listening to our conversation "she told herself. She then turned suddenly to Eddie like a frightened dog in a cage.

"You see what I was trying to say? She went on. "I would not be able to manage the work and course together. I would have to give up the course, honest. I have to, so that I would concentrate on my job" she told him in a determined voice.

Eddie touched her left hand which she had placed close to her right leg. The soft tender touch sent shock waves into his brain. How soft and tender her hand was, he thought. "She was going to be my Madonna" he told himself. "She must" he insisted. It would be a real weakness on my part if she did not become my best friend. She was gentle, her voice soft and melodious like a nightingale.

"Talean" Eddie called out in a manly commanding voice. "You were not going to give up this course. I would give you all the support you needed. Trust me, we would study together, write the same essays. You were in a safe pair of hands as I told you before right through the year. There were students here who were worst than you.

She straightened herself, looked directly at Eddie. "If you said so, I would take your word for it. But I am not that clever, you know, I am more than a plank thick. You were clever. You had done all those degrees, and I have not.

But we would work together, you promise, didn't you?" she said with a smile and looking straight at Eddie eye to eye.

With a broad smile Eddie nodded his head twice.

Talean soothed Eddie's hand, trying to reassure her self as Mrs. Will. "I was right" she told herself

A fellow student came to join the conversation, and stood directly by Talean "You were Mrs. Hill, am I right said the man who stood before them in front of the desk. He was in his thirties and wearing a black suite, dark hair that looked like it had not been combed for a year. His hair was in small coils with white particles sticking out here and there. His voice was typical East African. He had a pair of black shoes that were both shinny and reflective. He walked with an unusual gait.

Talean turned round with a start and smiled to him. "You were alright" she offered her right hand. "I am Mrs. Will, I am very well thank you.

"You remembered me from yesterday. I accompanied you to the bus stop." He made a false smile, put both hands on the desk to support his weight. He tried to look into her eyes. "You got home alright yesterday?" He asked her. He pulled his hands close together to occupy Talean's full attention.

She relaxed into her chair to stop him from invading her private space

She tried to avoid his eyes, she sat back took her purse and fumbled with it as if she was looking for something. She kept on searching her purse then her hand bag. She replied "I got home alright" without looking at him. I had to change two buses. I had to wait for half an hour in the city center for the next bus the number 74 to Tipton.

She still avoided eye contact with the man. She continued searching her bag in pretence. It's hardly an hour from the University to where I live in Tipton, but if you have to change buses, that made the journey lasted a lot longer, nearly two hours and sometimes more than that.

"That was a long way away then, By the way my name is Obusah. I come from Malawi in East Africa. I forgot you first name.

"Talean" she replied reluctantly.

"Miss Talean" he repeated. He was not getting anywhere with the conversation. Talean was avoiding him and he got the message and walked away to join his brothers who were speaking in Swahili and soon joined in their conversation, as Talean made a side look to see if he had left, before she put her purse back in he bag and breath a sigh of relief. She made faces that showed a negative reaction to the man's uninvited and un welcomed intrusion.

CHAPTER 3

▼

Eddie sat quietly besides Talean behind the table. Talean was married, he thought. That could be the reason why she was upset when she touch my hand. But did it ever matter anyway, he asked himself. Nothing was wrong with that. But if it had been the other way round, ran my finger over her cheek or caress her hair; that would have been out of order. It was a mere body language show. He was not listening to her conversation with the man, and was not paying attention to what was going on between them. As soon as the man left, she turned round to Eddie.

"You alright Eddie?" she said in a raised voice. He woke up from the day dream. You friend was talking to you. She nudged him with her elbow. "You were sleeping or just ignoring him? she insisted.

"Non of that "he replied as he straightened himself. "I was not sleeping, I was just thinking about lots of things in our conversation. He turned round quickly to talk to his friend with a joking gesture and said with a broad smile the Professor's speech was too academic and not that interesting.

I am sorry Obusah, could you repeat what you just said, I was not listening to you, I was actually cranking my brains on something else. I was sort of living in Gu gu land, You get what I mean. I was in another world away from here, I am barely looking through you and not at you and so excuse me for not hearing what you said.

Obusah sat opposite Eddie on the table. He supported his head with both hands, and his elbows rested on the table. It made him looked straight at Talean.

"You came from the other side of Africa?" Eddie asked. "Your accent was East African I could tell. We have different accent all together.

"Yes, I come from Malawi Obusah replied as he shuffled his feet.

Obusah looked at Eddie. "I have seen you around but I have not had the opportunity to talk to you. You came from West Africa, I supposed from your accent." Obusah said in a calm voice. Your accent was very strong and authoritative, it was also rather heavy.

Eddie looked at Obusah with a keen eye, and then looked at Talean.

"Yes. I came from Magburaka in Sierra Leone. It's a town in the center of the country. It was equidistant from any direction, North, South, West and East Obusah scratched his fore head slightly. He was trying to figure out where exactly the country was in West Africa. "It's near the Gold Coast?" Obusah asked, after a short silence.

"No man, it's on the C shaped part of the map of West Africa'

Talean joined in with her absolute ignorance of the Geography of Africa, but with intent to contribute to the conversation.

I had never actually looked at the map of Africa" she said with a smile. But I think that Sierra Leone was near Israel and Ethiopia. That was where the Rastafara came from. Haile Salasie was the living God of Rastafara"

"Hmmm, that was too far away from where I came from" Said Eddie.

"It's near Nigeria then? I had a friend who came from Nigeria. She was very nice and liked cooking. We always had good time together. She used to tell me about her customs, how to respect men and the traditional beliefs. The marriage customs and family hierarchy in her culture," Talean said.

We could go into the library and look it up in the atlas, Obusah suggested, but no one was interested in going into the library.

"I would bring a map of Africa and show you exactly where I came from," Eddie promised, then looked out through the window into the cloudy sky and the fast moving clouds, then the tall tower, in the center of the campus.

Talean still baffled by her not knowing the geography of Africa added "Africa must be very big I suppose. Excuse me with my ignorance of our ancestral land. We only know about Africa from the pictures we saw or the pictures we saw on the telly. All about wars, famine, disease and starvation, and people dying of malnutrition were all that we knew about Africa."

Obusah looked at Talean with eyes of admiration. "You must have been living here for a long time?" He told Talean.

She looked up and smiled. "No, not really" she replied. I came here on an exchange program, somewhere in London for one year. I was invited to come here and head the day center. I was not an administrator before. I thought I could do this course so that I got to know what I was doing and be able to do it better."

Eddie shuffled his feet, and then pulled them closer. He put his hands on his knees, pulled his shoulders up and then looked at her with an eye of importance. He said in a low but proud voice" I have done administration for five years and postgraduate diploma as well. So this was just an addition to what I already knew. I have had first hand knowledge of administration. I might not learn anything really new. It will be sort of an extension of my knowledge on the field and what I have already learned.

Obusah nodded with an eye of approval, not that of admiration. "You should be able to give a helping hand in my job won't you?" Talean asked.

Of course, I should, if you invited me to your day care center to help with the paper work.

Eddie smiled and nodded his head. He felt some air of importance blowing through him. It was all falling in place he assured himself, as he glanced at his gold plated watch. It gave him an added beauty spot. He felt pleased with himself. He smiled and fell back in his chair. "I am in charge," he told himself.

"I will surely come to the center to help.

"That was very nice of you" Talean said with a broad smile." You will be able to meet all my staff, lovely and hard working young women. They were all experienced and very inviting.

Obusah was not sure what to say. He straightened himself, and then waved both hands by making a sign of the cross. He got up folded his mouth into an O shape. He looked at Eddie, then turned round and walked away.

Eddie held his breath and laughed inside himself. He knew that he had won the day. He said to Talean "could I accompany you to the bus stop?'

"Oh, please do, you have to see me get on the bus of course. I do not want to be raped on the way, would you like that to happen to me?" she looked at him direct There were a lot of strange things that were going on in this society all the time, which Eddie never heard of in Africa. He had never heard of a woman been raped on the street, in her house, in public squares, the killing of people like bush animals was un heard of in his home country in West Africa. This must be a violent society he thought with all the stuff that was going on all the time.

The hall was now half empty. Most of the lecturers had left and the students were going out one by one or in pairs. Loud noises could still be heard round the hall as students and lecturers continue to acquaint themselves.

Talean glanced at her watch, she shouted "Oh gush, its past nine o'clock already. I wouldn't get home until after eleven pm, if I caught a bus after nine pm, I should be able to get home on time. Come lets get to the bus stop quick" She took his hand and pulled him to the door. She was walking so fast that Eddie had to take little skipping steps now and again to keep up with her. Talean could not see the funny side of the situation as Eddie tried to keep up with her fast steps. When Eddie spoke behind her and out of tune, she realized with startling surprise that Eddie was not listening to her properly. She nudged him with her elbow to get him to listen to her, not realizing that he was almost out of breath.

CHAPTER 4

▼

Eddie and Talean were walking down the road to the bus stop. The Professor's speech did not impress Eddie. He was expecting an individual introduction of students and tutors. But the speech was not only boring; it was long, winding and too academic. "May be it was intended to scar some students away from the course, since they said the course was intended for white English students only." The pair slowed down as more and more students streamed in both directions of the narrow pavements down the road. "I am sorry for dragging you out into the cold she said to Eddie who was having a hard time keeping up with Talean who had long legs and took long strides against Eddie who was short and took relatively short strides and so he needed to double his strides to keep up with Talean

Talean looked on her side at Eddie, trotting behind her. His black cap was pulled over his ears. They walked past a lamp post. She saw the way his Adam's apple was bubbling furiously above his high collar

"This man was very kind," she thought, walking me to the bus stop on a cold winter night. She stopped and looked at Eddie. "I am truly sorry Eddie, but I have to walk fast to catch the bus." She squeezed his hand in sympathy. And to her surprise, he covered her hand with his own second hand, which was neatly gloved. He held her so tightly that there was nothing she could do but to continue walking. They both walked hand in hand.

"I lived in a hostel down the road, not far from here, "he told her. "We shared a kitchen, dinning room and facilities but I spend a lot of time in my room.

Talean tried to disengage her hand but she could not. He held her hand firm.

Linked together, they walked past another lamp post. Talean could see that despite the bitter cold, Eddie's face was beaded with perspiration.

I was a headmaster of a catholic secondary school for five years before coming over for further studies. I moved over here as soon as I completed the post graduate studies at Leeds University in Yorkshire.

Talean added "you were on study leave then I suppose and would be going back to your job after you completed the course?" She looked at him briefly'

"It's a period of rest for me actually after working so hard for five years without leave." He replied still holding onto her.

She nodded, and wriggled her hand once more to free it from his firm grip but she could not. She breathed a sigh of relief as they approach the bus stop. A bus was coming down towards them from a distance. "It's my bus, just on time. You will be alright Eddie won't you? "She asked Eddie, as she pulled her hand free. She sooth her hand for a second and she could feel the numbness going away from her fingers. She could now feel the blood flowing again into her relaxed fingers. "Boy" she said to herself as her hand got back to normal "Thank you sir, it's very kind of you to see me on the bus. I thought you were a real gentleman. I would have been scared, honest being new in the place and having to walk alone down here to catch the bus. I wonder what could have happened to me, in the night and in a strange place with all strangers. She looked at him for a second, smiled and then jumped into the bus waving to him.

He waved back with a broad smile. He watched the bus driver closed the doors and Talean climbed to the top deck. The bus pulled away. Eddie crossed the road into a blind alley leading to his hostel.

He opened the front door of the hostel, walked upstairs into his bedroom without taking notice of anything and anybody. He did not even remember the flight of stairs to the first floor. He opened his room door quickly and entered his room, then kicked off the shoes from his feet in a hurry. He undressed, and for the first time he let his trousers fell and he jumped out of them like a child. He was singing inside his mind an old church song. He felt elated, he was not tired, but he was preparing himself for an early bed, when the door rattled a bit. He jumped with a start.

In came Kofi, one of the hostel residents. He was in his thirties. He had a bearded face and of medium height and average weight. "Hi Eddie! You had a good time today? You looked quite happy weren't you? You must have been doing something very interesting wasn't it?"

"Sort of," he replied. "Did I look really happy?" Eddie asked.

"Yes, you did, of course. Tell me what you did today. I was told you had your induction today?

"We had a reception actually in the Faculty, and I was talking to this lady from Jamaica. She was" Eddie folded his fingers into an O shape. "I have just seen her off on the bus."

Eddie looked ever more pleased with himself. He got off the bed and tried to dance.

"Waa oh! You hit the jack pot already. You must be a super man plus. Kofi told him jokingly.

"No man, not quite as you put it. We just had good talk, something of the sort. Nothing quite dramatic, Eddie said in a calm condescending voice. She was a nice woman though, friendly and out going. I thought we would get on along. She and I were going to study together anyway and write our assignments together, and did all the course work together in here? Kofi asked.

No man, not exactly in here, but we will be working together. She was a head-mistress of a day care center some where in the city. God knew where.

Kofi now seated on the chair facing Eddie listened with curiosity.

"Where were you going to be studying together, in your room, at her home or at the University?

Eddie was not prepared to give any more details. He hesitated, looked up the ceiling and out of the window. "We have not given that idea a thought yet, you know. It's too early to decide on a meeting place. But I should think that will be any one of the three places. Sometime in mine and sometime in hers, I should think" Why did he want to know these details? He asked himself. He should not be asking those details just yet. We were going to study anyway I would not mind where. Those were things that would fall in place with time, he told himself.

"Could I turn the telly on? Kofi asked.

"Oh yes, if you wanted to please do. I forgot all about it.

"I could not afford one just yet. I spent a lot of time in the common room lis-tening to news" Kofi told Eddie.

CHAPTER 5

▼

It was early in the evening, Eddie was trying to dose off when suddenly he was awaken by a loud slamming of a door. He lifted his head up from the pillow to listen to what was going on. The stream of people going into and out of the toilet and the noises they make woke him up. He lay his head on the pillow again. He looked blankly across the room. He tried to make out what was really going on outside his room. Its time to go to sleep, he told himself. He was still half asleep. But the noises and the opening and closing of doors, prevented him from going back to sleep. He tried to remember what happened earlier in the evening, but his mind was still asleep. Then the name Talean came to his mind. He would not recollect what went on with Talean. He then tried to think of what he had to do later in the day. There were faint noises on the foot of the stairs leading to the second floor. As the noises on the stairs sipping into his room got much stronger, somebody tapped at his door. He then decided to get up, and sat near the pillow. He looked at the bed, a single bed with purple curtains. He pulled himself to rest his back on the wall, using one of the pillows to cushion his back against the wall. He heard a faint knock on his door a second time. The door open slowly and in came Obusah quietly.

"Hi, Eddie, you alright?" he asked without looking at Eddie in the face. He sat down on the side of the bed with both hands on the bed like some one sitting reluctantly.

"Sort of" replied Eddie as he pushed himself towards the edge of the bed by Obusah. He put the pillow that was behind his back on his laps and both hands resting on it. He was slightly irritated because Obusah was trying to compete with him only a short while ago but he did not show it. Obusah was his contender and he left them in a rude manner after he found out that he was not a prospective suitor and Eddie was not quite sure what Obusah had on his sleeves this time.

"I have been in the living room watching some programs on the telly. I have not done anything except preparing myself a small dinner, Obusah told Eddie.

Eddie remained motionless. He watched Obusah with a sleepy corner eye. This man had been watching us all through the reception. Why was he coming into my room at this time? What did he want anyway? He asked himself. I did not like him anyway. I saw him trying to take my food from my drawer the other day, and when I scolded him, he told me he was only looking for something in my drawer and not his. The other time he was using my milk from the fridge and he told me that, that was his milk. Only when I showed him my name on the bottle, he said sorry to me.

Eddie looked quite disturbed on the inside, but he remained calm, with the pillow still on his laps and hands still resting on it Obusah did not look at Eddie on the face as it was customary not to look at people direct in the face.

You were a real hero in the arena today, he said sarcastically, I have come to congratulate you the chief and head of the manor, he went on jokingly.

"I did not understand what you were talking about" Eddie stormed.

"I have not been a hero, have I? What have I done to be a hero? "Eddie shuffled his feet, put the pillow away and moved to the far edge of the bed.

Obusah was still laughing and rocking on the chair. "Be honest man, you had the opportunity to talk to that beautiful woman. Did you know that every one was eyeing her in the hall including, Lecturers. You were a very bold man and courageous as well. I salute you for that" he got up and saluted Eddie like an army officer saluting his senior.

Eddie was completely over taken by surprise at Obusah's comment. "We were all mesmerized by her beauty and immaculate dress. But that was not out of the ordinary. I only happen to sit next to her by chance and we started talking as was always the case. We had common concerns about the course and everything that had to do with the program and how we were going to work at it. I was just building bridges so that I will complete the course successfully. But nothing unusual I *suppose. I am surprise to hear that every one was watching us. I was pretty certain that she could have talked to anyone else besides me if anyone else wanted to talk to here. So what was the big deal anyway?*

Who wanted to talk to her anyway? We were both strangers and out of the blue, we came to sit side by side by chance, Eddie said in a defensive voice. The woman was married. I was just making friends with her. You were trying to paint a picture that did not exist as far as I was concern" he went on.

Eddie changed his sitting position. He was now sitting face to face with Obusah with his left foot stretched on the bed and his right foot resting on the carpet and both his hands on his laps.

Obusah had changed his sitting position too. He turned round to face Eddie, and now sat with his right leg folded on the bed, his other foot hanging over the chair's arm, and he was fiddling with his collar. He surveyed the room. It's a small room just enough for a small bed and a small reading table by the head side of the bed. Above the table was a small book shelf. The clothes cupboard was besides the bed on the foot side, big enough to hold half a dozen clothes hangers. Eddie put his box on top of the cupboard and his shoes behind the door.

Obusah looked at Eddie briefly then in a cautionary voice asked, "Have you known this lady before," still looking at Eddie.

"No, not really, but I have met lots of West Indians women before" replied Eddie.

Obusah cleared his throat; then asked again "so you already knew the formula for dealing with these people. He looked at Eddie then out through the window as one expecting the answer to come from the clouds.

"Well, I guess I have some idea of how to start a conversation with them." He said in a confident voice and relaxed facial expression.

*Obusah, could not quite make out what Eddie said. Eddie knew the customs of these people and how to approach them, Obusah told himself. "I wish I knew the formula before. I should have been talking to her instead of him. I was very stupid not to have sat next to her the moment she came in. I came in before Eddie and the lady. There was lots of room beside her, but I was a bit timid, honest, I was, Obusah told himself. I h*ave never talked to a woman out of the blues. The other thing was if I had gone to sit next to her, she might have got up and move to another seat which would have been more embarrassing to me, he told himself. I was very well dressed, may be she would not have moved, if I had only tried. I never made the effort, it was all my fault, stupid me," Obusah blamed himself. He sat down quietly looking through the window like someone listening for a distant call through the air.

Obusah was still silent and looking through the window, when Eddie turned to him suddenly and said in a loud voice.

"Are you day dreaming?" Eddie asked.

Obusah turned round quickly to look at Eddie. He smiled, "I was not day dreaming, no, I was thinking about something that happened the other day that I could not remember quite well. I was digging my mind to get at it."

The evening was wearing thin and Eddie was dosing off. He stopped talking; his head was in a sleeping position. Obusah kept talking without looking at Eddie. He was still looking out into the dark. The building had gone quiet. Eddie's telly had been turned off. Obusah's head was now resting on the table in a relaxed position.

The door opened quietly. "wake up Obusah and go to your bed," said Kofi who just came in for a quick chat.

"What were you wondering about, your wife and family?" he asked Obusah. You better start forgetting about them, because you will not be seeing them until sometime next year. That land of yours would remain unexplored for one whole year, you better stop wondering about a missed event, no one was going to explore that land behind you, and she would preserve it for your return." Kofi laughed loudly. Eddie lifted his head up, looked at Kofi like watching a clown displaying.

"He was thinking about his wife, may be someone was having a go at her. Kofi said jokingly with a big laughter. Eddie could not resist laughing, he joined in the laughter. Obusah thought these men were making fun of a true story that could be happening at home behind his back, He thought it was not funny at all and not something to make fun of.

Eddie looked at Kofi, shook his head and they both laughed again. Obusah's voice was shaky as he tried to reply. Eddie and Kofi continued to laugh at Obusah's crocky voice, a sign of guilt and accepting the reality. Obusah looked angry as his body language was suggesting. His face twisted and his mouth tightly folded inwards. Obusah got up and without saying another word left the room. He walked down the stairs, across the hall, up into his room and locked the door behind him.

Obusah must have been irritated that was why he left abruptly and with out saying good night or even a word, Kofi said jokingly.

Kofi you have touch on a sensitive issue, you know, Eddie said in a scolding voice. He could not bear to laugh at our folly about his wife, but he had mixed feeling about the idea, I bet you. "You were right you know anything could happen behind his back. Women were gullible; they were easily persuaded by false pretences. If some man told them that you were going to get married here to a white women, they would believe it, honest. I knew a woman who two of her relatives came here to study and they both took back wives with them. They got married to white women. "Eddie told Kofi. These men had wives and children back in Africa. They abandon their African families for the white women. It was ever so sad, when a man came here and forgot about the struggling family he left behind by pretending to be single and take up another wife. It was a sin many of our country men who came here before us had committed and still went back home and live.

"My brother did that he took a white woman back to Ghana" said Kofi. "I would not be surprised, if one or two of us who came took back home a white women. I will never marry to a white woman, no way. Honest." Kofi added. "I do not mind the experience which I think was good and one would understand and would accept as a genuine mistake for the sake of it."

"Why not," Eddie added. It did not hurt and did no harm to play around while you were here and make the best of what was available to you.

"There will be trouble in my family if I did go home with a white woman. I take care of my parents. They were now too old to work. My relatives came and went. An African woman would understand that my old parents need her help. Our women knew that by looking after the relatives they strengthen their marriage bonds. But this did not exist here with the white woman. She did not believe in extended family systems. She believes in husband and wife only."

"But you could tell her about your customs before you get married. If she loved you she would accept it Eddie told Kofi. Many African men have got married here and had gone home to live happily over there with their wives and the extended family around them. It really depended on you the man that was my opinion" said Kofi. He then cleared his throat, then he went on but would you not like to have a go if you had the opportunity?He asked.

In a quick and straight forward answer Kofi answered "off course why not. You may not want to miss the opportunity and the experience."

"Of course not in a million years, why would you want to miss a golden opportunity?" Kofi repeated. "I cannot keep this bag overflowing indefinitely, you know. I need to empty it from time to time. But these white women do not want to talk to you, you know. They appeared to be in a hurry all the time. Even when you try to talk to them, they would not say nothing to you. You were not really sure if they liked you or not. It borders me sometimes when you stop to say hello to someone and they just walked on. Sometimes they appeared to hurry up the moment you try to talk to one of them. I did not like someone ignoring me, when I did not have bad intentions, but may be they think that every black man was the same. We were all evil men. That could be the reason why they were afraid of us and do not want to talk to us. I love to have a go if I got the chance to do so. It was an adventure I have never taken and might never come upon again if

I missed it this time. I think it would be a shame on any one of us to come to this country for one year without that experience. You get what I mean?"

"It's worth having that rare exposure, I should think," Eddie answered.

But Kofi, you cannot sit in your room and expect the white sheep to be delivered by an angel for slaughter in your room, do you?" Eddie told him. He looked into his face for an answer, and then went on. "You needed to visit places like pubs and clubs and talk to people. You need to start a conversation with someone, or join in a conversation."

Kofi shuffled his feet; put his right foot on top of the left under the chair. "I have been to pubs, you know. But it was not as easy as you were saying it here now. Nobody ever said hello to you. I did not know how to start a conversation when nobody said nothing to you. When they look at you like someone from another planet, an alien of some sort. Where did you start the conversation with someone like that? That was the problem.

Eddie looked at Kofi with sympathetic eyes. "I see what you mean. But you have to realize that English people do not like strangers generally. They felt shy and insecure when they came in close contact with you, and they were very poor at starting a conversation especially when they did not know you. They would rather hide their face behind a magazine or news paper rather than talk to you. You had to break the ice, talk to them may be start with a joke of some kind."

Kofi was fiddling with Eddie's album. He was paying little attention to the conversation. His eyes catch the picture of a beautiful woman. "Waa ooh' he exclaimed. "Was this your wife Eddie? A beautiful woman this one was.

Eddie moved round to look at the picture.

Kofi took out the picture from the album, held it in his hand. "This photo reminded me of a woman I knew many years ago when I was still at school, the wife of Pa Matuala. She was the head wife. He was the village elder, with so beautiful women that every one envied him. He was beaten by a snake and died. It was said that Pa Adebola the village trader, planned Pa matuala's death long before so that he could have his beautiful wives, and was just waiting for the opportunity.

When a snake bit Pa Mutuala, he went into coma because he was hungry and tired. Pa Adebola ordered that Pa Matuala be buried immediately before night fall, according to village customs. There was again rumor that they heard sounds coming from the grave. They went to dig the man back in the dark, and found him sweating in the grave. But he eventually died a few hours later." All the wives of Pa Matuala married to Pa Adebola the trader.

Kofi took the picture from Eddie, looked at it closely. "This picture reminded me of some lady I knew long time ago" he said in a low voice.

That was a stranger you knew, because she was Olu's mum" Eddie told him.

"I must be day dreaming, because I did not know nothing about your country. I mean she resembled some woman I knew long time ago" Kofi corrected himself.

"She looked like this lady in the photo, but she could not be the woman I knew who was now an old woman. But you could still see traces of past beauty behind her weather beaten and wrinkled face. She was a real beauty, she was, honest." he added.

"Were you saying that my baby mother was not beautiful?" Eddie asked. He was already snuggling into his Duvet. He was feeling a little tired.

Kofi turned round to ask Eddie another question. He looked at the clock first then Eddie. He opened his mouth but said nothing. "Oh you were in bed already. I am sorry, but I wanted to ask you another question about this lady in the picture. But I better be going and leave you alone and go to sleep. It was time to leave, it was getting really late, the whole resident was quiet and time to get out of here.

Eddie threw away the duvet and sat up straight. "No, no man, I am not rushing you out. Please stay. I am feeling a bit cold that was all. The heater had gone off. You know that they turn off the central heating at 11.30 p.m. each night.

Obusah turned round and looked at the clock on Eddie's table just in time for the midnight ding dung.

"You see what I mean?" Kofi said to Eddie. Its midnight and I have kept your company up to the end of the day, and its now time to go to my bed. Let me get out of here before Mrs. Willie turn off the corridor lights. The man left, and he closed the door behind him.

As he left the room, Eddie drew his duvet and he was so sleepy that he hardly had time to say good night to Kofi. He went into deep sleep.

CHAPTER 6

▼

It was 7.30 am when Eddie woke up, with a start and hardly remembering what happened before he went to bed. He got up, stretched himself. He looked at the clock which had just gone 7.45 a.m. The album was still on the table. "What was this diary doing here? He asked himself. The chair was in the middle of the room and the door ajar. "Flipping heck, what was I doing last night, I never closed the door last night. He jumped up from the bed to check if everything was alright. He looked round in a hurry, and then checked his pockets to see if anything was missing.

"Oh Kofi and Obusah were here last night." he laughed at himself after his memory had rekindled. "Wait, did I see them off? Oh dam it, they must have left because I was too sleepy and it was past bed time. That could be the reason why the door was not closed. He tiptoed into the toilet. As he opened the door from the outside, Obusah was pushing it from the inside to get out.

Eddie pulled his face away quickly to avoid been hit right on the forehead.

"I am sorry, "Obusah said to Eddie, standing face to face. They were both holding the door handles, one on the outside the other on the inside. "The door did not hit you though?" Obusah exclaimed in a smiling voice.

"No" Eddie replied. "Guess what, I found the door half open and the chair in the middle of the room and I was totally confused as to what I was doing last night. I just came to my senses now and realized that you lot were in my room late last night. I must have been very tired not to remember to lock the door." He walked passed Obusah quickly as someone else was coming up the stairs to use the toilet.

"We could see that you were falling asleep, that was why we decided to leave you alone and get your sleep.

Obusah moved out of the door to the side, to allow the students to go in and out of the toilet. The traffic to the toilet was getting more crowded

"You were going to the University this morning?" Obusah asked. He stood with his right foot on the stair, holding on to the wooden stair case rail.

"Off course, we have our first lecture this morning at 10.00 am."

Obusah changed his position, shifting his weight to the right leg. "Your friend will be there as well?" he enquired.

Eddie lifted his head, looked away. "Well, I should think so. We were doing the same course." He replied in a soft voice.

"I could not remember her name you know. She told me her name the day we accompanied her to the bus stop. I did ask her name at the reception yet again. She must have thought that I am a fool to ask for her name every time I met her."

"Talean" Eddie replied in a calm voice.

Mrs. Talean was it?"

"No, Talean Hill" We address people by their first name, not in Africa where we address you as Mr. or Mrs. She was Mrs. Talean Hill. I got it now thanks" Obusah said. "How could a Mrs. befriend a man here? It's a bit strange wasn't it. That was not right, was it?" he said to himself. "You were going to be good friends weren't you Eddie?" He asked jokingly in a loud voice. He made a sarcastic laugh, as he nudged Eddie with his elbow. Obusah moved to the toilet door, held it open for Eddie and made a sign for him to go in.

Eddie changed his countenance. It's an expensive joke he thought and decided not to say anything. He walked into the toilet; his body language was that of defensive posture but did not look round at Obusah.

Obusah watched Eddie go into the toilet. He observed the changed attitude in Eddie's reaction to the remark. He knew that Eddie was now upset with him. The sarcastic remark had made Eddie upset, but he controlled his anger and decided not to say a word.

Obusah seeing that Eddie had changed his countenance quickly said "I did not mean to offend you. I was just pulling your leg. Sorry, if I upset you."

Eddie stopped, looked at Obusah for a while, with cold looks "I am not upset" Eddie replied in a sharp tone. "I just wanted to get into the loo. My bladder was filled and I needed the toilet before anyone else came in." He positioned himself at the door such that no one could go through before him.

"Alright then, I would let you go and use the toilet. I would see you in the kitchen. He let go the door and walked away.

"Alright dear," Eddie rushed into the toilet holding his breath. He tip toed and forcefully drew his Pajamas zip. He squeezed his dick to stop the urine already trickling down his fingers. As Eddie breath down, he nearly missed the loo as his bladder could no longer hold out the urine. "I made it but just, as he looked at the drops on the floor tiles. The door opened suddenly, Eddie jumped and remembered that he had not locked the door.

"Sorry" said Yeomi. "Quick man I am pressed. This was the only toilet for all of us. I did not know why they have only one toilet for more than a dozen men. Yeomi walked out and stood by the door outside. He had his right hand on the door nub, and half his weight on the wall.

"I would soon come out "Eddie shouted to Yeomi.

Eddie rushed out, knowing that Yeomi too was pressed and needed to use the toilet soon. I knew what it meant to be pressed for a wee man. I have just had a near disaster, but it was these fellows that were holding me up on stupid conversation.

Yeomi tip toed into the toilet. He already had his trousers half way down to his knees. He closed the door with a bang.

Eddie forgot to wipe the wee on the tiles. He could hear Yeomi from outside like the sound of popcorn in a frying pan.

Eddie walked back into his room to get ready to go to the University. He looked round, and then dressed up in a hurry. He took his folder together with the pen and then made a quick glance at the mirror. He hurried down to the kitchen to make his breakfast. The kitchen was spacious, with long kitchen tables and a row of industrial cookers and refrigerators. Student food cabinets hang over the table

CHAPTER 7

▼

The kitchen was spacious, with very old long wooden kitchen tables and a row of Industrial cookers that have already out lived their usefulness and colonial Fridges. A row of outdated wooden student food cabinets that looked like preserved museum furniture hung over the tables. Eddie walked into the kitchen quietly. The kitchen was half full with students, making breakfast. The smell of fried bacon, eggs and sausages filled the kitchen. Eddie stood for a while, hardly knew what he was going to eat for breakfast. He then walked to the big Fridge, opened it. All the items in the fridge were labeled with student names. He took the plastic milk bottle with his name on it. He held the bottle at eye level, and then walked away with it to his food cabinet. He took out the sugar bottle, put it under his right arm pit, then took out the cornflakes and poured them on the plate. He held the plate and milk and walked slowly to the dinning table. The first three tables were full, he looked round and there were two empty spaces on the forth table. He walked across to the forth table, put his plate down, milk and sat down opposite two young ladies. He made his breakfast plate. He looked round the table to see who was sitting on the same table. He took the first spoon and with out looking, he missed the mouth and poured some of the milk on the table, which drained down to the floor.

"Oh, oh, what were you doing Eddie? Were you still asleep? Wake up" shouted Kofi. "It seemed you were not with us on this table. Your mind must be far away from here." he went on.

The table was now fully occupied, as the last space on the dinner table was taken up by another man. They all stopped eating, turned round to look at Eddie. He got up, went to get tea towel to wipe off the milk.

"I will clean up this mess on the table for you while you clean the floor" offered the young lady sitting directly opposite him. "What was bordering you this early morning? It was not a good beginning of the day, was it? You were eating like a baby, messy," she said as she wiped off the table. She looked at Eddie who was now busy eating his breakfast.

The lady took her tea towel and handed it to him.

"Thank you" he said as he received the tea towel. He went into the kitchen with the bowl of corn flakes, still half full. He drained off the milk into the sink and the corn flakes into the bin.

What were you doing shouted the lady frying eggs for break fast? She asked Eddie as she looked at him with folded mouth.

The lady looked on with awe as Eddie emptied the bowl into the bin.

Dumping all of that?" the lady asked in a scolding voice. "What a man you were wasting all that food.

Eddie looked at her, felt guilty of his act, but he had already dumped the corn flakes. He looked into the bin for a few second, and then looked at the lady again. "They did not taste good" he told her. He felt a big bobble going down his throat. He held his throat in a chocking position.

Eddie walked back into the dinning hall, sat in his seat, took his tea cup and he took a sip from it, without saying a word. He picked up the tea the second time and his left hand were still shaking. He almost dropped the tea cup again. He put it down quickly. "Oh God" he said to himself. "What was this? What was going on this morning?"

Obusah who was sitting at the far end of the table eating his breakfast shouted out, you alright? He was watching Eddie from his seat. "I have been watching your behavior for a while. You seem nervy this morning. What was troubling you? You had the best of evening Yesterday. You should have been cheering us up this morning. What happened to you? You must be thinking of the negative side of what went on last night, or you were having a night mare or something," he asked in a joking voice.

Eddie sat still for a short while and then put his hands under his chin to support his head. "I am alright; it's just that my head was a bit cranky.

Eddie sat still for a short while and then put his hands under his chin to support his head. "I am alright; it's just that my head was a bit jerky this morning. I do not know why," he replied in a soft voice.

Obusah cleared his throat jokingly. "You were fretting man" he said in a low sarcastic voice.

Eddie's countenance changed. He sat in a defensive posture. "Fretting about what?" Eddie asked in an angry voice. "I am not scared of nothing. I did a post Graduate Diploma at Leeds University last year, you know. It has nothing to do with my studies. It's just natural that sometimes you wake up in a buoyant mode and sometimes you wake up in a miserable mode. It's just one of them things. It happens to lots of people, man. "He took a sip of his tea slowly, looked far away. He could not still understand why he was nervy. As he got up from the table, he could feel his left leg tightening up. He sat down again. His leg was shaking violently, as he tried to control it and maintain a calm posture. I am going to get up and go up into my room, he told himself. He got up from the long bench, held the table for support, moved his right leg across the bench, still holding on to the table. He walked away slowly.

Obusah watched, but said nothing. Some of the students had left the table already.

He walked awkwardly away from the table. "I am fine, I am just having a bit of cramps on' my left thigh, otherwise nothing was wrong with me "he told Obusah who was watching with some concern. He went up the stair case slowly, holding the wooden rail with both hands on either side. He could hear his heart beating loudly. Tired and breathless he entered his room, sat on the side of the bed. "What was going on?" he asked himself.

Eddie walked through the double glass doors into the main foyer of the School of Education building. He turned left, went up the three steps and stopped to read the notices.

A soft touch on his right shoulder he turned round, and he almost kissed Talean who stood so close behind him that her breasts were almost touching his shoulders. They both laughed. She looked into his eyes. They were full of passion and love.

She smiled, and then pushed her face forward, she pulled it back quickly. "No," she told him. She looked round, put her hands over her open mouth. "I am going crazy" she told him. "I am losing control of myself. I was going to, you got what I mean? She said in a shy voice. She melted, then folded her hands before her lap and made shy maneuvers.

Eddie watched with amazement "You were alright?" he assured her.

"You knew what I was going to do?" she asked him.

"Yes" he replied with a sharp voice. "That would have been lovely" he said in a warm voice.

She pushed her shoulders up in a distasteful manner. "Nooo" she shouted in a low voice. "I could not do that in a public place like this. I have never done that before. But I loved to do that, you get what I mean? You were a man, you do not care. Women were shy, they preferred the man took the initiative" she told him.

Eddie looked at her for a while speechless. "How did you get behind me? It seemed as if you were from no where. I did not see you coming" he exclaimed.

She giggled, then said" I tiptoed to surprise you. You enjoyed the reception last night? I did, honest; I thought it was great, with all them speeches. I had the best evening for years. I have to be honest; you made it a good evening and a day to remember. You get what I mean.

Eddie's face brightened up with smiles. "Oh, so you enjoyed my company then? I thought I was awkward with you last night." He smiled and looked round the foyer which was empty.

"You had to excuse me for trying to blow my top last night," Talean moved one step backward as she spoke. She occasionally looked round the foyer, as if she was not sure of whether she was behaving right or not.

Eddie had now relaxed and in a buoyant mode. He rubbed his hands together often. He transferred his folder from his right armpit to his left. "I have no complaint about your behavior last night; you were a perfect woman every man should be proud of. Lots of eyes were on you. You were the most elegant student in the hall.

"Were you really serious? "She asked with an enquiring voice. "I did not realize that people were looking at me and admiring me. I am just a black woman like any one else. You get what I mean?"

"I thought you were a very attractive woman. You should expect to attract attention.

"Oh shut up, you were flattering me. I am not that attractive" she said in a deep voice. "I knew that people were watching me, and that was why I was a bit upset. I did not want people to watch what I was doing" she said as she touched Eddie's shoulder. "I was a bit shy, you get what I mean." She smiled and looked round.

"I thought every one was talking at the same time. How come people were watching me? Was it because I was the only black woman in the hall? I was definitely sure that no one was listening to our conversation.

"Ya man, no one was listening to us. We were talking in low voices, besides lots of people were talking at the same time. Nobody could have heard what we were saying, honest. We were not saying anything out of order, were we?' He rocked forward in a reassuring manner.

"I hoped so" she replied smiling. She looked at Eddie with relaxed eyes, then she opened her eyes wide.

"Thank you Eddie for reassuring me. I thought I made a bad first impression of myself. I had that feeling up to this morning. But I now felt alright I felt really pleased when you thought that our conversation was alright and no one else heard us. Thank you" she said as she moved into the lift.

CHAPTER 8

▼

It was early morning. Eddie got dressed up and left for the university. He walked out and went up the road. He walked pass the bank play grounds onto Bristol Road. The road was still clear with few cars moving in both directions.

Eddie got to the School of Education. He looked up the tall building. "I was a bit early into the faculty building" he told himself. He was not expecting to meet any one there. "I must be an early bird this morning" he thought. He walked through the two sets of double glass doors into the foyer.

Talean sat on the wooden bench directly opposite the doors. She saw Eddie coming in through the glass doors, she smiled.

"I thought I was an early bird," he said as he came towards her.

"No man, I have been here for some time now. I got a bus as soon as I left my house and got to Dudley Road. In the city center, I met the fast bus just ready to move. I got on it and got here too soon. Besides I was a bit nervous. I did not know what to expect, so I decided to be here early enough just in case I missed the lecture room. I thought that if I got here early and missed the room, I would have enough time to get there before the start of the lecture. It would not tell well to be late the first day. I went to the day center and told them that I was coming for a lecture. How were you anyway?" she got up and stood by him. Talean sat down again. Eddie put his folder on the bench and sat by her. He looked at her then smiled. "I am alright. She put her blue folder on her laps.

"You were really ready for the start of the course I presume," Eddie said as he inspected Talean's folder.

"She smiled. "I am, of course. I have paid a lot of money for the course. There was no point dragging my feet about it. You were on a scholarship right? You would be given another chance if you did not reach the standard. That opportunity did not exist for me. I would lose all the money I paid for the whole year.

Eddie saw Obusah coming through the glass doors. He walked straight towards them, and with a broad smile he said "Hi Eddie and Talean. You were ready for the battle of the books?" He held his folder under his right armpit. Kofi appeared suddenly from no where. He joined the group with broad smiles. Talean turned round suddenly. Her mouth was wide open but she was lost for words like a person caught red handed doing some mischief. She shuffled her feet, straightened herself and took a defensive position.

Eddie stood motionless for a moment as if he was looking for words to say.

Obusah moved towards the lift. "Are you lot coming into the lift?' he asked. Obusah stood close to the lift and made invitation gestures to enter the now open lift.

Eddie looked at the wall clock just above the lift as it struck 9.00 am.

"Yes we are" Eddie replied. "Come on then" he beckoned to Talean. "Quick" he told her.

Obusah went into the lift, held the door open for Eddie, and others to come in.

Talean looked round, smiled, and then followed Eddie into the lift. He beckoned to her to go in first. "After you" he told her with a smile and a stretched of his right hand into the lift.

"Thanks. You were a real gentleman. It's hard to find a real gentleman these days, especially when women were asking for equality of treatment. I am a woman and wanted to be recognized and treated as a woman." She folded her hands across her Tommy, looked around and then Eddie. She moved closer to Eddie.

"But that did not include giving women preferences in public places which was generally acceptable"

Kofi said in a low but confident voice.

Obusah turned round to Eddie "Who did we have this morning?" He asked.

"I am not too sure who was lecturing this course, you know" Eddie replied. "But I think it would be Professor George." he added.

"Oh yes, I knew him" Talean said in a quick and sharp voice." It was he who welcomed us yesterday

I am sure about that and he was a nice man. I liked him. I enjoyed his speech last night." Talean moved very close to Eddie, held onto his coat by the shoulder as she was squashed. The sweet smell of her arm pit poured on Eddie's hunger and thirst for her. "You were wearing a sweet smelling perfume there," he whispered into her left ear, as he turned his head to reach her ear.

She pushed his head slightly and put her index finger on her lips, telling him to shut up. "Behave yourself. We were in a public place." She rounded her mouth into a small shape. She then folded her arms across her chest. She took a step backwards and then looked up at the lift electronic counter, and the number seven appeared.

"Here we are" said Obusah in a loud voice, as the doors opened.

Eddie moved out first, stepped aside, and then held his hand for Talean to come out. She held his hand and jumped out. "Oh gush," she said. "I did not like these things you know. They scared me to death. I prefer to go up the stairs." She protested in a soft voice.

"Never mind" Eddie replied as he led the way into room 744.

"I would see you lot later" Obusah shouted and walked fast towards double glass doors, without waiting for an answer. He walked with quick steps through the double glass doors, and into the long corridor and disappeared into the maize of rooms.

"Tra" Talean said in a raised voice to Obusah after she freed her hand from Eddie without looking round. He let go her hand abruptly. She soothed her hand as if it was squeezed out of blood.

Talean emerged first from the lecture room. She breathed a sigh of relief. Without looking behind, she walked to the lift, pressed the call button. Eddie who was actually following behind moved closer to her to make way for Mr Ivon who had just come out of the lecture room and was also waiting for the lift to go down. More and more students gathered around the lift doors.

Mr Ivon turned to Talean who stood close to him after he shuffled the mass of papers in his hands, "was the lecture alright?" he asked.

"Yes" Talean replied in a sharp and confident voice, with a smile. She tried not to attract attention to herself. "That was good. I enjoyed every bit of it. He was eloquent and knew the stuff to his finger tips. He was really good,"

Mr. Ivon shifted his weight from left to the right foot. "Well, he would not be sitting on that chair if he was not. Those were the qualities they looked for in appointing people to that position of responsibility. The ability to lead and knowing what you call stuff well.

Eddie showed signs of indifference. He ran his right index finger through a list of names and titles.

He pretended to hear but not really wanting to take part in the conversation. He said to himself "this was the man who told me that because I am black, I could not do this course. He said it was too hard for me to go through success-fully. I have promised myself that I would tell him in the end that he was wrong in his assumption. I would certainly remind him he was racist for sure but not just yet but on the last day of the course. He was racist, down right racist. How could you tell the ability of a man based on his color only?" he was in his own world.

"Oh put that paper away for now Eddie "Talean told him as she pulled his hand away from the white sheet with tiny prints. "You did not even say nothing about the lecture. You never even supported what I was saying. I am sure you were impressed by the lecture and the stuff that was examined." she looked at him .

Eddie was still motionless and appeared passive and he was still in his imaginary world. He raised his head and looked at Talean in the face. She smiled, put her right hand on his shoulder. "Are you alright?" she asked.

Eddie nodded without smiling back. "What an awkward man you are.

CHAPTER 9

▼

Talean's face looked tense with anger. She walked briskly with her head high and her mouth folded to a long. Eddie realized that something was wrong. He walked behind her. She knew that Eddie was following behind but she did not look back. She doubled her steps with her head in an angry posture. He called out but she did not stop or turn round. They walked into the library.

Eddie walked closed behind her, and caught up with her. She walked on without taking notice of him.

She stopped suddenly. Looked round at him with angry eyes and without saying a word, flicked her head, and then walked on.

"Hey, what was going on here?" he asked in a raised voice.

Talean stopped, put her right hand under her left armpit. "I am not talking to you again. You Ignored me" she snapped, then walked passed him, avoiding his shoulder. They both walked in silence into the library. Talean ignored Eddie and walked to the far end of the library. She put her bag on the table, sat down forcefully. She turned her eyes away towards the book selves. "How would I find the book I need in this mass of books" she thought.

Eddie came up the stairs, looked round and ended at her. He then walked slowly towards the table.

Talean knew that he was coming but she pretended not to hear him coming, she turned away, to avoid eye contact with him. He sat down opposite her, took a deep breath and then said to her.

"Look here Talean, I was not trying to ignore you. But when that man came close by and he was talking to you, my blood ran chills. He was dam right racist. It was him who told me that the course was designed for white students and that he did not think; I would be able to go through the course successfully. I hated him and so I avoided talking to him. I was by no means avoiding you but I was not in a mode to talk to him either and the fact that he was talking to you I thought I should stay back. I am sorry about that." He made a false smile first, and then pulled up his eye brows. He then looked at her with a broad smile. "We would get on well you know," he continued "We have been put together to discuss and work on the same projects. We could not avoid each other could we? I am interested in you and your welfare. I would look after you right through the course," he told her.

She shook her shoulders. "If you said so" she replied, as she drew her feet under her seat. She crossed her arms on the table to support her body. "I felt a bit funny in the man's eyes because I was looking for support from you. I expected you to support what I was saying to him. You have to be a hypocrite to survive in this place. Things were not always going right to expectations. So you have to tune up yourself to the beat of the day. Otherwise you will never get what you wanted. You always needed to wear that hypocrite laugh on your face and make false smile when ever you met these people. Remember that hypocrites were the ones that won the day. It was a fact that if you try to be too honest with people or too outspoken, your future would always look blick. You knew very well that these people could fail you and you would have nothing to do about it and no one to complain to. You better keep your feelings to yourself at the moment or until you completed your studies here. This was England the country of the white man. Did you believe that you could still fail no matter how hard you worked, if these folks decided to fail you? You better take it easy man with these folks. You better join the company of hypocrites like everyone else, just to get what you wanted," she looked down.

Eddie got up looked up in the ceiling, took the book list, had a brief look at it, and then walked to the book stacks. As Eddie looked through the reference list, he nodded his head in support of what Talean said.. He raised his head, smiled and looked at Talean in the eye. "You were right love" he said softly.

"Love!" she repeated in a deep, surprised voice. "I was not your love. We were just friends. We did not know each other very much yet. She frowned her face and looked upset. "But this was Yorkshire English. It has no specific meaning. It's a market language in Leeds City." He said in a quiet voice. He smiled, put the paper on the table, and then looked at her.

"I am sorry, you were right my dear. I have heard this language before. I should not have thought it other wise." She put her right hand into her mouth for a while, then folded her arms across her chest and sat back in her seat. She then folded her lower lip inwards.

"I liked to see you smiling dear," he told her in a joke.

She pulled her head back suddenly, looked at him, "That sounds better," she said smiling.

She pushed her face forward on the table and spoke softly, but in a determined voice.

"You have to realize that there was a barrier between us, you know" She used her hand to divide the table between them. "This was my personal space; you could not and should not cross this barrier.

Get that straight into your head now. If for any reasons you tried to cross this barrier at any time eh, the response would be unpleasant, do not try it, no way. Not now for any reasons, if at all." She moved her head left to right slowly. She then pulled her legs back and relaxed into her seat and looked straight into his eyes for reaction. She pulled her mouth together and sat still.

Eddie remained motionless. "What is this woman up to?" he asked himself. "I have not done any thing out of order. Lost for words, he looked at the paper on the table lying between them. He raised his head slowly and looked at her.

She was testing the waters, I suppose. She had put the cards on the table I guess. I should grab the Jack, I am the man. "Alright, I got you now. You looked more beautiful when you were serious, honest. He looked at her smiling.

What a beautiful woman you are?" he laughed. She twisted herself without saying a word.

She pretended not to hear what he said at first. She ignored his praises, made her face more serious and went ahead and fiddle with her bag like looking for something. She was not looking at him even though she knew that he was directly looking at her. She could feel his eyes on her face as she looked into her bag.

He continued to look at her. She smiled, lifted her head and looked at him. "Did you really think so, even when I was upset? She said softly.

I looked like a monster at the best of times, believe it or not, honest" she told him.

"No man, you were not, you never looked like a monster. You got even prettier when you were really serious" he said in a smiling voice.

She was a bit confused. "I was trying to ward him off, but it was having an opposite effect. May be he was interested in me" she told herself. "I would give him a tough time before I tell him my mind. She was interrupted by a female student who just came by and asked for help to get a book. Edie got up and went to help her.

He came back a short while later, sat down. "I have never seen so beautiful a woman like you for a long time, honest.

Believe it or not, it was really true" he told her in a low joking voice.

"Oh shut up, stupid full, do not flatter me. I am not that beautiful, I did not deserve those words, reserved for special women." She looked at him, screwed her eyes, and looked at him again with soft eyes like someone looking for fine details on an object of interest.

"You were very special didn't you think so? Eddie asked her.

"Stop it now" she pointed her finger before his face. Don't get excited, we were here for a purpose and let us get on with it right now, she said in a commanding voice.

I have to go back to my job, you know. So we have not got all day to sit here and talk about stupid things that went into your mind. You better behaved before I thumb your face.

Talean was now excited, her face full of smiles as Eddie praises her beauty. "I am not that pretty she said to herself. "I wished I was that pretty, I would have done modeling. When I was a school girl I attended dancing classes, and I was doing modeling as well, you know." Mr. Delroy told me that I had the features of a model girl. I kept thinking about it for a long time, but the idea faded out when I failed to go to high school, because my parents had no money and I did not win a scholarship. I was attending a special school which I did not like. I was going to a model school secretly, but I was coming home late each day and my mother discovered. I was given a good beating. My mum said model girls were called wore because that was their trade and I hated been called by that name and so I decided to quit modeling.

Eddie was listening attentively at the same time trying to locate the books they need. He was making funny noises as he listened and looked through the book stacks.

Talean came close to him, but he did not notice her behind him and so he went on making the noises. She tried to hide her excitement from her recollections of her past life. "Oh shut up and got on with what you were doing" she said to him in a surprised voice. "I needed just one book for now to read tonight" she told him.

Eddie looked round, her face was just an inch from his, he smiled and then walked away to the other stack.

She went back to sit down. He looked at the index box while he kept an eye on Talean at the far end of the table. She sat quietly. "I wonder what she was thinking about. She looked like a dolly from a distance. He walked up to her and said "you should come over and help me or watch what I was doing and stop day dreaming about your job and your childhood.

The words ran out from his mouth like the voice of a nightingale in the dead of night. She looked up at him, smiled and said nothing. She got up, made her scat

He turned round and then remembered that he had left his wallet and keys on the book self.

And without waiting for a word from her he walked back quickly to the stack to collect his keys.

He came back quickly to the index box.

Talean got up, put her bag on her left shoulder and walked towards him.

"You were right Eddie; I needed to learn how to find the books I needed on my own. But why did you not wait for me?

Why do you keep going back and forth to the index box? You naughty man" she nudge him on the shoulder softly. "We could walk together, you know. Don't you run away from me; I did not smell bad did I?

Some men would be proud to walk with me. I knew that for sure." She stood behind Eddie and watched what he was doing.

Eddie turned round to look at her. "Would you stop talking about your self, and watch what I was doing so that you would be able to find books" he spoke in a soft and controlled voice.

Talean moved one step closer, "I am watching. I have come closer and looking at the index cards with you" she said in a laughing voice. You could do two things together you know, talk and work, did you know that? She put her right hand on his shoulder. Eddie made no response.

"Alright, you did not want to hear my voice. I would not say one more word" she said. "Now tell me what you have done so far?" She looked into the index box and tried to read the names and titles.

"Oh yes, this was one of the authors on that list. Let me have a look at the list again." She took the list from Eddie's left hand, scan through it. As she ran her index finger through the Authors column, she stopped at Pollard, A. 1974. She went back into the index box. "Oh yes, I have found this title.

Give me a pen, let me copy the details. It's easy then, I thought it was something very hard to do. You were coming upstairs with me to look for the book in the book stacks?" She pulled Eddie's arm. "I wanted to look for another book for my self;" Eddie protested. "You needed one book and I need one as well."

"You come help me find this book first, then you can find one for yourself while I look through this book" she said in a begging voice.

Eddie raised his head and closed his eyes as if he was praying silently. He followed her up stairs

As he followed her behind, he looked at her shape from behind. She had an eye catching round bottom.

His mouth watered and his blood pressure went up.

She stopped close to the landing on the stairs to allow him to lead to the book stalls.

She looked down the stairs and saw him watching her. She smiled, and watched him with out saying a word. He walked on and stopped suddenly. He felt some sensation ran through his nerves.

He then walked passed her by squeezing through. He rubbed his shoulder on her breast. She looked into his eyes, and then said "you did not have to do that. There was plenty of room for you to pass by, naughty man. You behaved like a curious little boy she said in a scolding voice.

Eddie smiled and said "I wanted to smell the perfume you were wearing."

"Did it have anything to do with what we were up here for? You could smell it without squeezing my breast. This breast was a bit tender, you know." She held it with her left hand and bounced it lightly. Eddie's mouth watered again.

"Is it?" he asked. He turned round and faced Talean. He stretched his hand to hold her breast. She slapped his hand saying "stop it. You could not touch it." He looked at her "why not?" he asked forcefully and walked away.

"It did not make any difference if I did, did it?" he added without looking at her.

She frowned her face, screwed her mouth into a nut. "Yes it did" she replied. "They were not yours and for your to touch. I have told you that before. Haven't I? This space here was out of bounce to you." She used her hand to demonstrate the boundary again.

Eddie turned round to watch her mapping out the exclusion zone in her body that was out of bounce to Eddie. He was concentrating his eyes on her breasts which looked delicious and inviting.

"Stop looking into my breast, you little creep. I did not know what was getting into your head." She pulled her dress up to cover the bit of breast showing out which Eddie as gazing at.

A very delicious and delicate delicatessen he said to himself, as his appetite and thirst soured to its peak. His mind ran far and wide, but he tried to restrain himself. I needed to be a man, he told himself. "Hay, what was so important about that little space of yours. It would be mine someday" he said aloud. He put his hand over his mouth. I should not have said that. It's not nice to say that now. She might get frighten of me. Dirty big mouth I have. "I am sorry; it's a slip of tongue. I did not mean what I said. It just popped out" he said in a low conceding voice.

She looked at him with scolding eyes. "You have a big mouth didn't you. You speak first before you think. She folded her mouth; she pointed her finger at him and said "don't you dare think about stupid things. Don't you ever dream about it, you get what I mean. No way" she flashed her finger across his face. She turned round, moved a sew steps away and said in a commanding voice "let us find the book now and stop being stupid and naughty. You got that into your head; do not open your mouth and say anything."

Eddie turned round and walked towards the book stacks in silence. She followed him behind closely. He concentrated on looking for the book.

There was a muted silence. Eddie tried to think over what she said. She was lying, he told himself.

Every woman was like that they pretended a lot. They initially say no to test your determination. They soon give in if you persisted. I did not really think that she meant what she actually said openly.

I knew for sure that when a woman said no, she did not always mean that.

"Which way were we going? She asked, as she looked on either side of the stacks and it looked the same to her. Each stack was full of books neatly packed and in serial numbers.

CHAPTER 10

▼

It was late in the afternoon, Eddie and Talean were still in the library. She looked at her watch. It was past the hour four. She felt some emptiness in her Tommy. She looked out through the window, at the daylight coming in through the windows, and remembered that she had to go to the day center to be with the kids, to release Fay.

I did not think it made sense to go home and come back here tomorrow to get books out. She showed signs of impatience. Eddie realized that she was becoming impatient. She took the reference list out, looked at it, then walked to the window and then back to the stacks. "It's getting late you know. I have to go to the day care center, but I needed to go with one book to read tonight."

Looking for a book in these stacks was like looking for a needle in a hay stack. You were the only one that had the time to go through these stacks to get the book you needed. I was not wasting my time to look for any book at all. It looked so confusing to me. I was only watching you, but I was not going to go through any of these shelves."

"I was looking out for your book first. I would come back and look for mine later.

"Oh you were looking for the book by Pollard?" she asked. Eddie nodded his head. "You sure I was not been a pest on you back?" Eddie shook his head slightly without saying a word. "You sure about that?" she asked again in a joyous voice. She walked over to him; put her hand over his neck. She looked round to assure herself that no one was looking. "You were a nice man. I liked someone like you to work with. But it was not that easy to find the books you needed in these stacks.

"Well, if you have not used the system before it looked difficult. But if you got used to the system it looked simple. You just follow me right. I knew where we were going. We would soon find your book" he assured her

She looked at him and then made a broad smile and her face brightened. "Yes sir" she replied in a happy voice.

Eddie turned round to look at her as she replied in an unusual voice.

She smiled again, put her hand over her mouth, "you were the boss man. I should give you that respect, shouldn't I?" she asked him with a smile that impressed Eddie.

Without looking at her he said "that was very kind of you to call me sir. It was not easy for you to hear that word here. People here looked at each other as equals. Even Professors had told us to call then by their first names. That was how the society stressed equality as a social custom.

But I will not call any one of them by their first names. I am not used to that. In the West Indies, every one was called either Mr. or Mrs. Only children were called by their first names. In Africa too, we called people by their titles, as Mr. Mrs. or Dr. You never call an adult by their first name, it was an insult to the person, Eddie told her.

So how would I get used to calling lecturers by their first names.

"But they have told us not to call them Doctors or Professor.

We just have to tune up to the society's culture" Eddie told Talean. We would get used to it; we just have to dance to their tune. He came close to her, took her right hand and moved on. She followed him without asking a question.

"I would find it awkward to call these people by their first names, honest, but I would try and get use to it." She said in a low voice. She looked at Eddie as he scanned through the book titles one by one.

"Why not, we just have to do as the Romans did. I hope you were following the procedure as I tried to locate the book for you. I knew nothing what you were doing dear. I depended on you wholly for my survival, honest. I should give you that respect if nothing else. I planed to pay you for all the help you would be giving me through out the course. It's a hard course, I have been told, but I was determined to do it and graduate.

Eddie stopped turned round and looked at her. "Pay me?" he exclaimed. "I would not ask you to pay me for studying together. It made it easier for both of us if we studied together. The company alone was more than enough." He told her in a soft very low voice.

Talean moved closed to him "Oh you liked my company, didn't you?" she asked in a cheerful voice, "that was good to hear. I hoped you did not get bored with my company later on, as too much of one thing led to boredom. I would try not to be too demanding, as I some times asked for too much and expecting too much." You did not have to do all that I asked for. You knew women were too demanding and sometimes we made too many demands and expected too much. But never feel out of the way if you could not meet my demands, just say no and that would be it. I might kick a sting, but that should never worry you.

Eddie went back to scanning the books pretending to hear what she was saying. Talean looked away and said hello to a lady in the far end of the stacks who was busy looking through the stacks on her own.

"You were right Eddie, Talean replied, but I needed to give you something for your extra time. I meant to give you something, you know, honest. It was from the bottom of my heart. I felt obliged to do something as a token of appreciation; to make you really happy to help me."

"You intend to pay me really?" he asked without looking at her. He suddenly turned and looked at her. She nodded her head, while looking straight at him with half closed eyes. "What would you pay me? You pay me," he looked down at her round bottom and brown belt round her waist. His eyes caught up with her eyes as she lifted her head slowly up.

They both smiled. "I like that buckle" he pointed at the brown buckle on her scat. He tried to touch it. She knocked his hand off without saying a word.

"Could you stop surveying every inch of me, I did not like that, you know. Keep your hands to your self," she said in a soft and low voice.

Eddie moved back. "Alright sorry" let us get back to business.

"Here we are" He held the brown book high up in the air. "This was the book. Take it down and have it stamped," he told her.

She took the book looked at it, made a quick review. "Come with me man, o.k. You stayed with me until I got on the bus, and then you were free to do what you wanted to do alright?" she told him in a commanding voice. She walked behind him down the narrow stairs to the issuing desk.

As she put the book into her bag, she said "come with me to the bus stop.

They walked out of the library into the foyer in silence, then through the double glass doors into the street and down the walk way past the student union building.

Talean led the way while Eddie followed close behind. Talean looked back to see if Eddie was following.

"I am here" he assured her. She waited for him to walk by her side

"You were coming back into the library after I have gone on the bus?" she asked.

"No man, I am going home. I have to cook my dinner.

"Oh dear, you had no body to prepare your dinner. We lived in a hostel. We prepared our meals." he told her.

"I am lucky" she said as she stopped to wait for Eddie. "I ate lunch at the day care center, then my Aunt prepared dinner which I just warmed up and eat when I got home in the evening. Men could not cook. I would prepare a dinner for you some day" she looked at him. "Would you like me to cook for you sometime?" she asked in a cautious tone

"Yes, of course" he answered with certainty and vigor. "But where?" he asked.

"Where ever," she replied. "At you hostel, I supposed." she said as they walked slowly down the hill past the bank to the bus stop.

"That sounded nice, the students would call you Mrs. Eddie Buwanda." he told her.

"Nonsense, that is. You have to be married to a woman before she could be called a Mrs." she said in a sharp tone. "I would tell them that we were just friends," she told him.

"Did you know that a woman had to be your wife or girlfriend before she could cook for you? That was the belief of Africans. But it was not always the case. Some people lived forever without getting married. If a woman was your good friend she could cook for you. Boyfriend and girlfriend living together would do cooking together wouldn't they? I hoped the hostel people would not mind. They did not allow us to bring women friends or alcohol into the hostel.

"How could they? You were adults and not kids. That sounded daft. They were doing this because you were Africans and would accept any condition. Did you yourself accept that condition" she asked?"

Eddie remained silent. They walked on "Did it matter if we.... .? She looked at him with soft eyes. "Oh, there was my bus coming. Come quick" she said as she ran to the bus stop, holding Eddie's hand and forcing him to run with her.

"You come to the day care center Thursday. Would you? We would have lunch at the center."

Without waiting for an answer, she jumped into the bus, walked to the back. She sat down and waved to Eddie who waved back. She kept looking behind until the bus disappeared. Eddie waited for the moving traffic before crossing the road to go back to the hostel.

CHAPTER 11

▼

It was late in the afternoon when Eddie crossed the road. Eddie walked fast as it was getting cold and frosty. He opened the door and walked straight to the stairs. He went into his room in silence.

His mind was blank. He had a cold air of peace and contentment blew over him. The work was going to be so easy and straight forward, he thought. He had a quick glance at his table. Hs room was in disarray with books and papers all over the room. He looked round the mess in his room and hardly knew where to begin sorting his work out. "Let these books stay right where they were for now" he told himself. He had a peckish feeling. "I needed a cuppa" he thought. I must go to the kitchen to make a nice cup of tea. He kicked his shoes off his feet. "I would do this when I came back. He went into his sleepers and left the room in a hurry. He walked down the stairs slowly. The place was quiet except the sound of music from the room upstairs and some noise seeping out from the matron's sitting room. He walked through the hall without looking round. Every where was quiet. Students had come back from the University, but were in their rooms. He walked passed the empty dinning hall into the kitchen He stood by the gas fire. Dumb as if blind folded. "What was I going to do? He asked himself.

His mind was still blank. Suddenly the thought came to him as if he was reminded of what he should be doing. "Oh yes, a cup of tea first, he told himself. I am dying of thirst" he told himself.

Mrs. Osborne the matron walked into the kitchen with a white cloth in her hands. As she cleaned the fourth stove at the far end of the kitchen she said to Eddie "you had a good day? I supposed the first day at the University was had, finding your way round and tuning yourself up to the routine of things.

She moved to the stove next to where Eddie was boiling his tea water in a large blower kettle. "I have never been to college, but when I started this job, some fifteen years ago. I still remembered how hard it was to get to know where things were, how to organize the use of these four stoves by over thirty students, both males and females. Some of them had never cooked before or even washed a dish. It was absolute chaos at the beginning managing so many people, some adults were coming to cook for themselves for the first time in their lives and it took me ages to develop the routines. I knew it was always difficult at the start of anything. She stood close to Eddie. She wanted to clean the stove Eddie was using, she watch him prepared his tea. I am getting these stoves ready she said, for the evening when most of the students were coming to prepare their meals. Some of the girls would be here soon to do their cooking first before the men came in.

"It was not too bad today," Eddie replied. "We had only one lecture today."

"You already met some one you knew before or made friends with some other African students?"

"Well, sort of" he replied.

"You will soon get friends, I am sure. She stopped to look at Eddie in the face. "I tell you, this was a very lonesome place. You needed friends to talk to and some one to go out with some time; otherwise it would be a boring to death place. Were you married or something and expecting your partner to come and join you?"

"No, not actually" he replied.

"Well," she said. "Its too cold here to sleep all on your own all the time. You will definitely need a friend, you get what I mean" She shook her head, put her hands over her breast, and then walked away.

"Yes" 'he replied without lifting his head. "But people did not want to talk to you" he said. "They ignored you all the time. So how would you talk to some one who ignored you and does not have time to stop and talk to you" he added in an upset voice.

"That was right, but you have to start a conversation with them. If you did not, they would not say nothing to you. We did mot like stranger and we" she pointed to her white skin, could not start a conversation with a stranger.

"It's you" pointing to Eddie who should engage us in a conversation. When you went to pubs and clubs, and you saw some one you were interested in, you would go near her and talked to her. She would respond if she was interested in you.

As Eddie poured the hot water into the tea cup, two girls came into the kitchen.

"Oh gush" one of them said. A young woman in her thirties in long grey dress walked into the kitchen quietly. "I am upset you know" she said to her friend in a sharp tone, who was in her forties, her face was a lot older. She had some unhappy wrinkles in her face. "That man was upsetting me, he kept talking to me, asking me all sorts of questions. I did not like him, but he kept talking to me and coming close to me. He tried to whisper into my ear. "What was he trying to do anyway, chat you up? You were young and beautiful. Every man would like to have a go at you." the older lady told her friend.

"Yes, I knew that, but he needed to be handsome and presentable, not a scruffy man like him." She looked around to see if Eddie was listening. She turned to her friend and laughed. She covered her mouth and showed signs of embarrassment.

Eddie pretended not to hear their conversation. He went on sipping his tea.

In came Julian quietly and stood a few feet from Eddie. The ladies did not notice him. "Did you hear their conversation?" he whispered into Eddie's ear. Eddie nodded his head but said no word.

The ladies looked at each other. "These men heard what we were saying. I thought there was only one man but there was two of them." "Hm there were two of them repeated the other lady."

"But I am still upset, the very thought of him made me sick to death. His mouth stinks like a skunk. Yeak. No woman would talk to him. It's good luck to have somebody talking to you the very first day you know, said the older lady.

"That was no good luck, its bad luck I thought, honest. He must wash his mouth first, change those old and scruffy clothes, she turned round again to look at the matron, Mrs. Osborne who was cleaning the kitchen tables. She pretended not to hear their conversation. Mrs. Osborne turned round in time to avoid eye contact with the young lady resting her hips in the table and folding her arms across her chest. Her weight was balanced on her left leg and her right food slightly bent inwards.

Mrs. Osborne went on cleaning the tops, and then turned round to face the lady, she smiled. The lady put her hand over her mouth; turned round and open her food cupboard. The conversation died down. She turned round to her Friend. They looked at each other; her friend nodded the yes answer and whispered.

"He was white, a flipping white man for that matter." She whispered into her friend's ear. "I did not like them lot, I hated them, they do not take regular baths. No way. The women were worst, they use lots of perfumes. He better look for a white woman of his kind she said in a deep contemptuous voice.

"But some of them were good looking you know" her friend told her. "They were neat and likable

"No man, I would have nothing to do with them. I hated these white folks. Honest. I just did not like them. I could not stand them you know.

"Have you ever been in regular contact with them?"

"No, not really" she replied.

Mrs. Osborne walked out of the kitchen quietly.

Eddie and his friend went into the dinning hall with his tea cup in hand and a packet of biscuits.

CHAPTER 12

▼

Eddie raised his head from the pillow. He tried to open his eyes, but was still feeling sleepy. It's Thursday today he told himself. I still needed a bit of sleep, but I could not because I would be late for lecture. He got up stretched himself, and then touched his fore head. He felt a bit of pain in the middle of the fore head. "Oh gush; I had too much beer last night. It's all Obusah's flipping fault. He kept buying and buying more beer, and you could not waste water in the desert." He went to his cupboard to look for Panodol. "May be I go to the toilet first, and then take two tablets of Panadol to fend of this pain.

He went out of his room to the toilet. Obusah was coming out of the toilet.

"You alright? Obusah asked.

"No man, I am having a splitting headache" He put his two hands to support the head.

"Hang over you mean? You need a full cup of cold water, and then tea. You will be alright after that" he told Eddie.

"Its all your flipping fault man, you kept serving me beer endlessly last night. No one wants to waste water in the middle of a desert.

Obusah laughed, "you were joking, weren't you? We were serving each other up to the end. Infact you bought the last drinks." Obusah ran downstairs into the kitchen, and came back with a cup of cold water. "This should do the trick" he told Eddie as he handed him the full cup of water.

Eddie took the cup of water into his room, put it on the table, he came back out.

Obusah was still standing by the toilet door.

Eddie went into the toilet without saying a word. He came out shortly after with his head hanging down like a sick man. He went into his room, sat on the bed lowered his head in a sick position. He got up to look for headache medicine. He took two Panadol tablets, held them, looked round, "may be I should go to the toilet again, before I take these tablets to fend off this pain, he told himself. He left the room again. Obusah was by his door, trying to come in. Obusah entered as Eddie was going out. "I soon come back, I needed to use the toilet again" he told Obusah. "I would take the Panadol with the water. Thank you Obusah" Eddie said as he walked into the toilet.

Eddie came back a few minutes later. Obusah was standing by the table in Eddie's room Eddie took the cup of water, threw the tablets into his mouth, then the water. He stopped drinking suddenly. "Oh, this water was too cold, it would crack my teeth, you know" he shouted.

"Oh come on, how would I know that, I took a cup of it before this one for you. Silly burger, that was the thank you, wasn't it? Always remember to take a glass of water first thing in the morning, if you had a hang over. It's the best anti dot. It would make you feel good and restore your energy."

He took the tablets and sat on the bed. "I am not cooking today" he said to himself. He took the bottle of oil and poured it in his hand to oil his hair.

Obusah turned round to look at him. "Why, were you fasting today? Besides, it was too early to think about cooking."

"I am going out for dinner." Eddie replied.

"Wow! Dinner already, where about? Obusah asked with a surprised voice.

"Some where in the city" Eddie replied with smiles all over his face and a feeling of importance.

Obusah looked at Eddie with surprised eyes. "Who invited you to dinner so soon? You had been anywhere yet and you were going out for dinner?"

Eddie got up the bed, walked to the mirror. "You knew who. Have a guess. I bet you knew who invited me.

Obusah scratched his head, twisted his face, and then looked up to the ceiling. "No" he replied. "I could not make it out. I did not know any one here yet. May be you knew many people and places here already"

Eddie rubbed his hand together. "Well, a big puzzle for you wasn't it. Let us go down and have our break fast, while you have a crack at the puzzle. They walked out Obusah first. Eddie closed the door behind him. Obusah was half way down the stairs. They walked in silence into the dinning hall, which was still empty, then into the kitchen.

"Invited to a dinner" Obusah repeated to himself. "How he could know people here so soon, a crafty little pig, he must be, Obusah thought. May be that beautiful woman he was talking to at the reception. "Oh yes, I saw then together in the library looking for books. "Ah, that was it" he tapped his forehead with his palm.

"Are you alright Obusah?" a young lady in her twenties asked. "You looked some what confused this morning. Are you sleep walking?"

Obusah dropped his hand, and then smiled. "I am alright, thanks. I am trying to recall some things that happened last night. I just got the answer. I have been cracking my head to find the answer," he said in a low voice.

"You got the answer now, haven't you?" she asked as she walked passed him smiling.

He tried to remember the day he went to accompany her to the bus stop, and he tried to take control of the situation. "Flipping bastard" he said aloud.

"Oh. oh," a lady near him said. "Excuse me."

Obusah looked round, frown his face and realize that the lady heard him. He looked at her, and then smiled. "I am sorry" he said in a soft voice.

"No need for that this morning in the kitchen. Your mouth was...." She looked at him and walked away quickly.

Well, I deserved this; I am a hungry wounded lion who swallow whole without chewing.

But I did not mind. I was trying to make a point. I hated him, he took that woman away from me I would kill him, if I saw both of them together. Honest. A nasty swine he was. Obusah walked into the dinning hall without carrying anything. He left his plate full of breakfast in the kitchen and tea cup. He was angry to the point of not knowing what he was doing.

Where was your food, the lady who heard him swear asked. She shook her head with disappointment.

He remembered that his hands were empty. He laughed at himself, and then went back into the kitchen.

He came a bit later with a bowl of milk and cornflakes and the plate. He was sitting down when Eddie walked out of the dinning room. Obusah did not notice the lady sitting next to him. He was still thinking about Eddie and his nasty tricks. He put his plate down and sat without eating. His mind was far away, as he looked into oblivion.

"Were you not eating your break fast? She asked, looking at him. He jumped with a start, and realized that he was being watched. He turned round and met with the lady's eyes, eye ball to eye ball. He turned the other way, and he was greeted with smiles. He realized that he was being sand witched by two ladies both watching him. "Flipping hell, why were these ladies watching me?"

"You alright, you had a bad night last night? Don't be a cat, mourning in the corner." the lady told him. "Did a lady turned you out last night? one of them asked. They both laughed. Obusah wanted to get up and move to the opposite side of the table.

"No man, you were not moving, sit down and tell us what happened last night. You needed to confess to us. We were women; we knew how a man behaved when a woman turns him down. Eat your breast fast and tell us the story," Said the lady on his right side.

Obusah sipped his tea slowly. "I have no story to tell you. I am alright." he told them. "So you were just thinking about the mistakes you made last night. You were coursing yourself then for not trying very hard and some one else took her away. Was that how it went?" they both laughed again.

"If you did not tell us, we have no advise to give you. But have our sympathy, and try harder next time. Have a nice day." They looked at each other. The lady on his left put her right hand on his shoulder.

Obusah was determined not to tell them anything. He pretended that he was just upset at himself.

May be I did not try harder that night he thought. I did not say a word to her in the first place.

That bastard, a little parrot did all that talking; never mind better luck next time" he heard a voice in the distance. But would there be a next time between me and him. He was already invited to dinner.

He closed his eyes for a while. When he opened his eyes, he was alone on the table.

The ladies had gone without his notice.

He tried not to think about what happened the other night. "It was supposed to be a night of disaster" he thought. "I lost the day" he conceded. "It could have been better, if I had put my mind to it. My brother gave me the first lesson on this occasion. On the other hand, I have never had a girlfriend. I had never faced a competition. I was given Mabella as a wife by my parents. I did not know that she was in love with me. I only knew that she was mad about me when I took her to the village ceremony. My mother brought her and handed her to me saying this was your wife, take care of her. We would over see the relationship she told me and that was it. So I have not had the Opportunity, to find my own woman Obusah told himself. I think it's hard to make relationships, especially if you came from the village where marriages were the business of the elders and not the youths to arrange.

Obusah looked round, the ladies were gone and no one around any more. He ate his breakfast quickly. He got up to go to the kitchen, and he took his right foot over the bench to move out, he faced Eddie who had come in and stood behind him. Eddie looked at him with searching eyes, but said nothing. He had his right hand folded under his left armpit; and the cup of tea on his left hand. He took a sip of his tea, looked around to see who was still eating their breakfast. He then looked at Obusah who sat quietly, "have you cracked the conundrum?" he asked Obusah. Eddie could feel the vibes of anger and angry looks from Obusah. Eddie noticed the body language of Obusah, closed his eyes for a second, and then walked to the door with out waiting for an answer. He took a few steps, turn round "have a nice day and enjoy your day" he said to Obusah, he walked through the door and out into the street on his way to the university.

Obusah who did not look at Eddie in the face, but had his face on his plate, appeared to be concentrating on his breakfast. Obusah heard Eddie, chewed his food swallow then replied "its alright, thank you." He sucked his teeth and then went on eating.

Eddie walked to the University. As he stopped at the traffic light, a bus pulled up at the bus stop, just a few yards from him on the double carriage way. He was joined by a large number of students who came with the Bus, and were going across the traffic light in a group. Talean came off the bus and stood close by him waiting to go across. He did not see her. She saw him first, she came and stood so close to him that if he turned round, he would go direct into her arms. He felt some soft breast on his shoulder, he tried to turn and her face was so close to his that she had to push her face back a little to avoid kissing him on the street. Eddie shouted with excitement "Oh you were here already?" he said with a big smile.

"Yes, I was trying to get here before you, to show you how prompt I could be and I did made it on time didn't I. "They moved to the corner near the wire fence away from the crowds of students streaming into the University. "I was trying to get here before you. I got up quite early this morning. Guess what, I was feeling a bit anxious, I do not know why. I left the house without finishing my breakfast. Do you sometimes feel anxious about some things? I was just over anxious about the course. I felt elated, and the fact that I had someone to help me with my studies." She stretched her body a little, melted away and then looked around. Most of the students had gone into their lecture rooms. "Lets go" Eddie told her as he led the way. "I didn't know why I felt a lot of anxiety inside me, this morning. If you were looking forward to an event, have you had the same feelings as I do now?

"Come on, the green light, let us get across quick." They joined the stream of people going crossing the walk way, holding her hand. They raced quickly across the second pedestrian crossing. He tried to pull her, but she resisted. "Don't" she shouted. He let go her hand in the crowd. "You got to watch the lights; those speeding drivers won't wait for you. I did not want to see you run over by a speeding car. It's too dangerous to run across the street after the lights were gone yellow.

They crossed safely although in a bit of hurry. "What have you been doing since Monday?" she asked, as they walked slowly up the hill past the bank "Oh, lots of things "Eddie replied. He looked up into the air, trying to remember the various activities. "A bit of reading, I went for an evening walk up to Sainsbury square. Last night we went to the trees pub. I am still having a head ache. We had a good time at the trees, video music, lots of students at the pub."

"Oh, you were drinking all night, last night? She asked, as she pulled him round to look into his eyes. She had a scolding face on, as she looked into his eyes. He smiled, "I am being serious" she said, twisting her face and biting her lower lip. "Tell me the truth" she said in a scolding voice. She was now holding both sides of his collar, without taking notice of the stream of students passing on either side of the pavement. She pushed him towards the hedge row fence, to allow students rushing up to the campus. Some students had a quick look at what was going on and then walked on, others stopped, but changed their minds and walked on. " Were you drinking all night, last night? Tell me the truth" she repeated. She let go his collar, as she pressed her Tommy and breast against him. He could feel the warmth transferring to his body. He could feel her heart beat as he squeezed his nose between her breasts. The sweet smell and freshness of her chest sent shock waves into his spine. His headache disappeared like magic. He could not resist the temptation, but took a few bites of her breast.

She jumped with screams of surprise. She looked round and realized that passing eyes were watching them.

"What you think you were doing?" She hit him slightly on the shoulder. "You don't" she hit him again. She opened her eyes wide, pushed her mouth forward and looked round again. "You drunkard" she said in a furious voice.

"No man, I did not drink a lot, you know. Besides that the pubs closed at eleven pm. You have to move out before they close. How could we drink all night if the pub closed one hour before midnight?

Think about it and try to reason things. We better go to our lecture.

She turned round and walked away quickly from him.

He ran after her to keep up with her pace.

She turned round and said "don't try that again, you naughty man. I thought you were a gentleman. You should behave yourself. I should not have to keep reminding you to behave.

I am not your." She looked at him with stern eyes, and without another word, she turned round and doubled her steps towards the education building..

She was upset, he told himself. "I did not do nothing wrong, and it was all her fault anyway.

He tried to walk by her side she crossed the road to the other side and walked with angry steps. "Did it hurt? I was just playing with you. I did not mean to hurt you. The freshness of your body made me to take a bit at your breast, just for fun and nothing else.

She stopped quickly, put her index finger over her lips, and she looked at him with cautionary eyes. I promised, I would not do it again. He told himself that if he had another opportunity by chance he would do it again. But I did like the smell and did not mind kissing your breasts again.

"Stop being stupid would you? That was foolish talk, you hear me" she said with raised voice. "These were not yours and could never be yours. Get that straight into your stupid head now.

Next time you try that I would box your face down. Do not try any stupid games with me," you see this? She folded her right fist into a ball. "You would get the full force of this on your flipping jaw." She demonstrated how she was going to send the blow. "I am very strong, you know. I could fight with any man. I used to defend my brothers and sisters at school. I was fighting for them all the time."

They walked on in silence for a short while.

Eddie listened with amazement. "You couldn't fight a man, not a man like me.

She stopped before him, looked into his eyes, with an imposing gesture.

"I would, you know, if I had to. I am not afraid of you.

They walked passed the two sets of double glass doors as Eddie held the doors for her smiling, as she walked passed into the foyer. They walked straight to the lift to join four other students waiting by the lift.

The lift doors opened, Eddie walked in first, and she followed close behind him. She stood close pressing her bottom against his belly. Was this deliberate? He thought. He could feel a current of heat transferring to his Tommy. She turned round and whispered into his left ear. "Please behave yourself alright"

They walked out of the lift towards the double wooden doors into the lecture hall.

Talean said to Eddie "guess what, I left the book at the day care center you know. I was in a hurry. I left it on my table.

"Never mind" Eddie assured her. We would work together.

She patted his left shoulder, saying "you were a good man, I am safe in your hands. " She walked with light heart and confidence, knowing that everything was going to be alright.

CHAPTER 13

▼

The day went fast, the lecture went on as expected, Professor Hays came in on time. He delivered a very interesting and easy to follow lecture on school management. The class was a mixture of students from developing countries, there were many students from developing countries and interesting enough we had a lot of African faces and some English students as well. They all sat as expected. The white students sat close together and the rest of the seats were occupied by overseas students as they were labeled. Eddie sat quietly listening and taking in what the professor was saying. He took notes at first, but stopped, and sat back listening. He kept an eye on Talean who was taking copious notes, page after page. He took the hand outs and the reading list. He made a quick glance at the reading list before they walked out.

"That was brilliant. It was a difficult subject made so simple. He tried to break it down into sub topics for us to understand. But I have to go over my notes to get the basic ideas he introduced" Talean said to Eddie as they walked through the doors.

"No new stuff was introduced. I have heard it all before in my diploma class at Leeds university. It was going to be just an extension of what we have done last year. It might not be as difficult as the Professor indicated to me at the interview. The end of a hard day, Talean said aloud. "Everything seemed difficult to understand and follow.

Would I be able to make it to the end?" she thought. "The beginning was always easy, but that was not the case here. I am lost right at the beginning. How would I be able to follow later, if I am lost now?.

More complex information and difficult to digest would be piling up on top of my day care work.

The future looked bleak. She was in deep thought when she tripped and nearly fall, excuse me; she held on to Eddie fast. He stopped and looked at her. She was dragging her feet, they seem heavy, and her head looked saturated. The neck seemed to barely managing the weight. She looked gloomy and confused, with signs of strain on her face. What was going on, are you alright?" he asked. She walked on much more slowly dragging her feet without answering. She was swinging her hand bag, and then put it on her left shoulder.

Eddie walked on her side. She walked on without taking notice of him. She stopped, looked at Eddie with confused and tired eyes.

"Oh Eddie, things look rather difficult for me you know," she said in a disappointing voice. "But I told you that there was nothing new in the lecture. Then you would have to explain all of it to me. I was totally lost," she said in a soft and down cast voice. You will not believe it, but I did not have the faintest idea of the exercises we did. And so was the rest of the lecture. It was all Greek to me. Let us run, the lift was here," she said as she pulled his hand. Then she let go his hand and ran to hold the doors. "Come in quick, and we would have it all to ourselves. The lift doors closed. She pulled his hand; she hesitated and then put her hand inside her mouth. The lift doors opened again and two men came in. She stamped her left foot and mourned. "Oh gush, we could not have this lift to ourselves even for a few minutes. She stretched her hand and held on the rail inside the lift. The lift doors opened again, Eddie came out first, and she followed.

"You were coming with me to the day center weren't you? She asked Eddie.

"Yes, of course" he replied with a confident voice.

"We would catch the bus to the city center, and then catch another bus to Handsworth. Dinner would be ready by the time we got there. You were stopping with me all afternoon. Were you prepared for that? She asked casually.

"Yea man, I think I am. I have been looking forward to this trip. Honest. I was thinking about it last night. I thought about you off course. It should be a nice afternoon with you I supposed and expected great things.

That was good then. I have told all the girls about you. They can't wait to meet you. They all have boyfriends though, so you should keep your mouth shut and do not wing an eye on any one of them.

They were beautiful girls for sue. I would watch all your movements, so that you did not try to make a pass word, or say something silly. Promise me that you will behave yourself. "Yea man, I am a gentleman. I would behave like one real gentleman, take my word for it.

"Here comes our bus." The bus pulled up and as the doors opened she walked into the bus followed by Eddie. Upstairs she told Eddie before she turned round and pointed him to the stairs. They got to the top, she sat down, and then he sat next to her. Eddie lifted his hand to open the window; she hit it slightly saying "keep your hands to your self."

"I was just opening the window" he said softly.

"What was that in your hand?" she asked. She pulled his hand to her lap. She took the bus ticket; put it in her purse, saying "I would keep it for you, alright?" Your hand is soft like a woman's hand.

Nervous and hesitatingly, she played with it. She opened and closed the fingers and rubbed her palm repeatedly on his. She looked at his face, smiled, she continued rubbing his palm. "You do not mind me playing with your hand, do you?"

"No man, not at all" he replied without looking at her but had a big smiling face.

"Your palm was softer than mine. I am a woman, you know, don't you? She lifted his hand, tried to kiss it, but pushed it away as she looked around to see if someone was watching. I wished we sat in this bus for one hour.

"One hour, where would we be going? He asked. "When I am going home in the evening I took one hour and fifteen minutes on the bus.

Eddie was looking through the window as the bus zoom down the road.

He has been on this bus several times but it seemed as if he was traveling on it for the first time.

He could not remember some of the familiar places he has been to. That was the Trees pub he said.

CHAPTER 14

▼

The bus stopped in a busy shopping center. They came off. Eddie looked round; the place looked strange to him, lots of Indians and no white or black people around. Eddie had never seen so many Indians in one place. They were moving in all directions, and across the busy street. "Was this part of India?" he asked himself.

He had not been any where before occupied just by Indians and very few black and white people.

This was not England I supposed. They walked on along the street and bend to a corner street. He looked at the street name on the side wall Soho Road. The houses were joined together like one long building, and lots of stores all occupied by Indian people it seemed. They bent the corner; he looked up again and saw the word Off License, he repeated the phrase. He tried to think of what they sold in the Off License store. He walked on still thinking about what went on inside this store. Then suddenly he saw a man coming out with a bottle of wine and a case of beer.

He realized that this was where they sold drinks. He looked across the street entrance and saw Linwood street. They walked down the street. The long endless building was divided into small houses, with the front door opening direct into the street pavement. Talean led the way. Indian after Indian they crossed on the pavement. The houses looked all the same except the paint and the number on the door. "How did these people identify their houses since they look very much alike" he said to himself.

This could be the reason why they called this country United Kingdom, because everything was identical.

"Your eyes were every where" Talean said to Eddie. "You have never seen these types of building.

Eddie shook his head. He was trying to make some land marks to remember in case he had to come back sometime.

"Well, all these houses were like that every where you go." She told him, and then she asked him to cross the street to the other side. Eddie tried to remember some land marks, but there was none. How could I remember this place? He thought. I am definitely looking for something to remember. I would certainly have to come back here alone. The only thing I have to remember was the Pump Tavern pub by the bus stop. He stopped and looked back along the street.

"Come on" Talean beckoned to him. I know you were looking for something to remember. I will show you what to look for when you come back next time. I would take you by the bus stop this evening and I would show you some land marks on Soho road. It was difficult to remember anything especially when you were coming here for the first time. "Am I going to stay here all afternoon?" he asked himself.

They walked on Talean led the way. Eddie looked at her gait. He forgot that he was walking in a raised pavement. He missed the pavement and stumbled into the street.

Talean stopped, turn round. "What were you doing boy?"

"I missed the pavement and nearly fell over.

"How come? You must have closed your eyes, or your mind was in a far away land,"

"Not really, I was watching your steps." He said in a low voice.

"Watching my steps, for what reason, I did not walk strange. You kept looking at me and you missed your steps. That was stupid wasn't it." She stopped looked at him. "Let's walk together. I did not want you to fall and break your leg." They walked together for a short distance. Talean made a sharp left turn to a foyer. It was all made of glass. She opened the door into the pouch. Eddie went in first, she then followed. They went through a brown door into a large rectangular parlor with a very large window. Eddie was greeted by a large photo of Marcus Garvey. Hence the name of the day center. Eddie looked at the photo. The man had revolutionary eyes, stocky build, and long beard in gray suit. He looked at the imposing photo more closely. This could be the founder of this place, he thought. The man in the photo seemed to look down on the people coming into the building.

They went through another door to a large hall half carpeted.

"Hi girls" Talean said to the three ladies serving dinner to the children sitting in four tables arranged in hexagonal.

"We go upstairs first" Talean said. She led the way through a U shaped stair case, round balcony.

The walls were covered with photos of black activists, black heroes and heroines. The most Prominent were those of Nelson Mandela, Martin Luther King, Malcolm X, Siaka Zulu, the Zulu warrior king. They went up steep stair case to the second floor. They were greeted again by an extra large photo of Marcus Garvey. Talean got to the landing; there were three doors close together on the landing. Both the left and right doors were ajar. The one directly opposite the landing was closed. She opened the middle door which was locked. She entered first, and then Eddie followed. A small room half filled with a table packed with files, books and assorted stationary.

As Talean sat on the brown revolving chair the telephone rang. She picked it up and beckoned to Eddie to sit down on the chair directly opposite her. "Its Ms Hilam, our food was ready.

She dropped the receiver, got up "I soon come back. I am going to bring our dinner from the Kitchen. She closed the door behind her. Eddie now had time to look round the room. His eyes first fell on a typewriter on a tiny table by the wall. Eddie got up to look through the side door.

He opened the door; there was a small metallic landing, brown with rust and metallic steps to the bottom of the building. Talean came in with a tray full of food.

"I am just looking at the fire escape," Eddie told her.

She put down the plates of typical West Indian meal of rice and peas and roasted chicken and Trefoils.

This was a lot of dinner" Eddie remarked. He received a plate full of brown rice, salted fish and two drumsticks.

"You were a black man weren't you; we ate a lot of food nearly all the time. You eat it all up." She cleared the table of papers and made room for him to put his plate. "You see what I inherited?" pointing to the masses of papers packed in piles, files and books all over the room. She cleared the rest of the papers dividing the plates of food. More papers piled up on top of the filing cabinet.

"The room looked more of a store than an office" she said in a disappointing voice. "This center had been going down in reputation for lack of a permanent head. That lot down stairs \were all NNEBS or nothing at all. They have no management experience. I did not have management experience either; but I have a teacher's certificate and a Diploma from Surrey University.

"Hmm, the dinner was good" Eddie murnured while he was busy eating up his dinner.

"You liked it? She asked.

Yea man, it's really good. I have not eaten a woman's cooking for ages." he told her in a surprised voice.

She stopped eating, looked at Eddie. "Haven't you? She asked. "What a shame. Ms Milam was a good cook. She had been cooking here for a decade now. I would take you downstairs to introduce you to the staff. Eat your trefoil, while I call for water.

As Talean took the phone to call the kitchen, Eddie ran his eyes behind the table. The wall was plastered with letters, memos, notes pined in such disorderly manner giving a mosaic pattern.

"Hello, Ms Milam, could you send us some water with a child please. Thanks"

She put down the phone. "I have not had the time to sort out any of these." She ran her hand round the room.

The door racked. "Come in" Talean shouted. "Oh Ms Milam why did you your self have to come up these stairs, you should have sent the water with one of them Picknies down stairs.

"You knew them stairs, not that good and them were not safe for pickinies to come up them stairs holding sothing, and me wan fe see the tranger as well." She said between heavy breathings.

"Oh Ms Milam, you were too good, you know, coming up them steep stairs. We were coming downstairs to introduce Eddie to you and the rest of the staff Eddie. This was Ms Milam our mother in the center. She cooked for us good dinner every day.

"A very good cook indeed" Eddie repeated, as he got up to shake her hand.

Did you enjoy the dinner?" she asked.

"I did very much" he replied. It's a very delicious dinner indeed. You saw my plate was empty. I ate all of it.

"It's good to hear that. You got joy when someone liked you cooking. There was some more in the kitchen." She said in a deep voice. She was breathing like a very tired over weight person. She was in her late fifties, broad chest slightly over weight about six feet tall. "Thank you Ms Milam, I am full up to here." He put his right hand under his chin.

"You did not mean that do you? You nor eat fe satisfy Talean?" Ms Milam said jokingly.

"No, no "Talean shouted, "I did not force him to eat all his dinner. I ate all mine, because I was hungry. He ate all the food in the plate, because he had not eaten food cooked by a woman for ages."

"Oh, oh, you nor have a woman?" She asked.

"He was a student at the University" Talean told Ms Milan.

Ms Milam transferred her weight to the left food. She seemed to have problem standing.

"What was that? she asked, The uni, univer, universiy" She gaggled as she tried to pronounce the name correctly.

University, Talean repeated. What was that " she asked again. "was it a school for old people?

"No Talean said "It's a college for adults."

Ms Milam looked up on the ceiling to try to make out what Talean had just said. "Ah, I got you now, a college. Don't use those big words. Me nor go better school, you know. Me own college was here in na the kitchen. Unu go college. Me cook for me husband." She was still breathing heavily, an indication of strain in climbing 28 stairs with her overweight body. "Mek me go down in na me hoffice, and lef una alone.

"We coming down in a minute Ms Milam" Talean told her.

She turn round, walked out closing the door behind her.

Talean looked up closed her eyes for a second. Nosey, these people are. She came to see what we were doing here" Talean said in a disgusting tone. She put the plates in the tray with upset behavior. She offered Eddie the cup of water in the tray.

"Thanks" Eddie said as he received the cup across the table. She was rearranging the table.

Eddie sipped the water with an anxious mind about the ladies downstairs. What would they think about Me. What impression would I make on them in the next minutes or two, when I got introduced to them? What impression had Ms Milam made of me? She was in her fifties, tall and stocky built, extra large chest and big buzz. No wonder she breaths like a fat pig. Her face was puffy, and of pale complexion.

Eddie got up and offered to take the tray downstairs, as he observed Talean struggling to balance the plates and the cups. "I would carry the tray, if you did not mind" he said to her with a smile.

Talean looked at him, smiled "Oh dear, that was very kind of you. I was wondering how I would get these plates safely downstairs. She took the cups from the tray and handed it to Eddie.

He took the tray with his left hand, opened the door with his right hand and beckoned to Talean to walk out first.

She walked out of the door slowly and majestically. "You were a special kind of man. honest" she said as she brush past him.

They were greeted by the imposing photo of Marcus Garvey again on the landing. "These were the things we believe in," she said as she took her time to walk down the stairs, holding on to the wooden rail. "There were black heroes and heroines." She stopped at the second large photo half way down the first set of stairs." This was the most famous of West Indian heroes. He was our patron. Our children all come from poor homes, with illiterate parents mostly single mums. They grew up without a role model.

These photos were to educate the kids on black consciousness, our history and black heroes."

They walked down and Eddie saw photo after photo of black people, including the Zulu King Siaka, Mandela. They walked into the kitchen. "This was our kitchen, this was our mother who cook us lovely dinner each day. The two industrial cookers stood side by side, clean and spotless.. A tumble washing machine in the corner beside the cookers was on. Its noise filled the kitchen. "We washed our children's clothes every day. Some of them have accidents now and again." Eddie was not familiar with the word accident in kids and was wondering how little kids like these would have accidents inside this place with the adults all around them.

Eddie went close to the pepper plant. "This was nice plant" he said as he played with the large leaves of the plant towering nearly four feet up the ceiling. "How did you get this plant to grow so big?" he asked.

Talean looked at Ms Milam first then Eddie with a smile she said "I did not know nothing about growing plants," she replied. "Ask Ms Milam.

"Well, I did no do nothing to it," she replied. "I brought the seedling from me yard and plant it, and me just give it some water now and again, Das all. Now it has some small peppers and flowers. Pepper plants were easy to grow, you know. " She walked to the plant, held the flowers and tried to smell them. She held the pepper pods delicately.

Talean said "she was very careful with things."

Eddie ran his eyes round the kitchen. A mosaic of food stuffs stacked high on shelf after shelf above the long kitchen table and over the cooking stoves and freezer. The food was packed according to variety. The biscuits were all on one shelf, the tined foods in two shelves. "There was a lot of food in this kitchen" he told himself. Why did they have so much food?" he asked himself. "This was a lot of food, wasn't it?" he said a loud. "You were right you know to some extent" she replied.

"This was the food we prepared for the kids each day. They have breakfast and lunch each day. Some of them get here very early and for some this was the only square meal each day. The parents did not give them a proper meal at home, so we had to give them a good meal before the end of the day." Talean told him.

"Das was not all" Ms Milam added.

"We stored some food in that room" Talean told him. She pointed to a door by the cookers, half closed.

We also kept some food upstairs in our store room. We did shopping once a month, and so we buy enough to last for the whole month." she told him, while she slowly walked away from the kitchen.

Eddie thanked Ms Milam for the food and the warm welcome, and then followed Talean. The dinning tables in triangular shape have now been packed neatly with the chairs in stacks by the window.

The children now sat quietly on the carpet, listening to a story been read to them by the youngest of the ladies. A medium build woman in her teens. Her hair neatly platted with large ear rings and all her fingers in both hands stacked with rings, and a ring stuck on her left nose. As she read the story, showing the pictures to the children now and again, her thick spongy lips moved like subsiding waves. "She looked pretty" Eddie told himself.

They came close to her, and she kept an eye on the kids, then on us and the book she was reading in her left hand, demonstrating with her right hand the events in the story.

The sound of foot steps on the stairs made Eddie and Talean look towards the staircase.. Three ladies were coming down the stairs, one behind the other. The ladies were all beautiful, well dressed, young and all in their twenties. "Its difficult to make a choice in this situation" Eddie told himself. All these ladies were beautiful and neatly dressed, but the one in the middle was an eye catcher. She was of medium build, round face, full of smiles and a convoluted neck. Her smooth face and crossed eyes and neatly platted head made her stand out. Her half split scat showed her smooth legs, were very inviting to any hungry wolf. They all showed the typical black woman's shape of round bottoms and sticking out breasts.

"Hmmm" Eddie murmured. He was now confused. Talean looked at Eddie to see his reaction.

He stood calm, saying nothing or does not know where to begin. His host was watching without saying a word. The ladies came close and stood by Ms Talean. They all smiled at Eddie.

"These were my ladies who work with me in this day care center." Talean told Eddie.

The lady stopped reading, watched Eddie.

His attention was on the three Ladies who just came in. He looked round and noticed that Talean was watching him. He remained motionless and stopped looking at the ladies. He turned to look at her, and their eyes met. She had inquisitive and hard looking eyes. She tightened her mouth and he remained motionless. They ladies all have typical African woman shape, round bottom and heavy breasts with sticking out tits like tiny ant molds. They waited in a semi circle until the third lady joined them.

Eddie's heart was beating like a little tom, tom. He could hear his heart beat . "I had never come face to face with so beautiful women together" he told himself. A range of different thoughts was going through his mind. Were they all married, some of them must be single, I suppose. But it was difficult to tell who had a partner and who has none, but hr could not ask at this point. He was deeply engrossed in this thought and he could not even hear their conversation.

"Hello Eddie" he heard the lady next to him on his right said. She stretched her hand for the hand shake with him. "Hello Jennifer," he replied. Her hand was warm and delicate. He could feel a heat wave going up his hand. Hello Fay and hello Anne Marie. He shook their hands briefly. They all turn round and headed towards the front door. "See you Ms Talean" the third lady to go out of the door still smiling said.

"They were going out for their break." Talean said to Eddie.

Eddie's eyes still followed the ladies, until they went out of the door.

Talean touched his shoulder softly; he then remembered that Talean was by his side.

"You were still thinking about those ladies eh? You would be seeing more of them later in the day. But do not start building castles of hope. I tell you now. They all have boyfriends," she told him.

"But what does that have to do with me? He said to himself, as they walked to the lady who had now completed reading the story to the kids. Eddie had a good look at this lady sitting with the kids. The door opened and a lady pushed in a boggy with a young child in it.

CHAPTER 15

▼

Talean walked to the middle of the kids, sitting in a circle. "I am coming to introduce this man to you kids. This is Mr. Eddie. He came from Africa and he is studying at the University. The children were excited. They sat attentively and anxiously, they looked at Eddie then Ms Talean. One boy shut his hand up quickly and he was attracting attention. Yes Miss he was still bouncing his hand for attention. Ms Talean looked at him, allowing him to speak out "did he wear leopard skin in Africa and danced with swords?" the boy asked. "My mum told me at home that Africans slept in caves and they wore leopard skins and slept in mud houses." Sit down Shady, Ms Talean said in a soft voice and ignored the question the boy asked. The children sat quietly, whispering to each other.

Eddie and Talean went upstairs. Eddie sat down near the type writer, while Ms Talean arranged her desk. The phone rang. She picked up the receiver; her face shown with smiles as she talked on the receiver. She then dropped the receiver, Eddie I am going to introduce you to someone who would need your help. She was a nice and beautiful woman. She was one of our mums. She has two girls in the day care. You have not met her but you must have seen her around sometime. Eddie swallowed with a big gulp. He was wondering who this lady might be. Lots of things were going across his mind, like scanning through a new video. Was she going to be pleasant? Eddie was thinking of many things since the first impression was always the most important encounter and all that followed would be the result of that encounter. He was in deep thought on how she would assess him, what impression would she have of him, and how she would appear to him, whether she would be lovable, or someone nice to talk to. Lots of questions were passing through his mind. He went into the toilet to look at his face and the way he dressed up. "I should look presentable" he told himself, as he looked into the mirror. The first impression he thought was definitely very important to both of them. It was the corner stone to any future relationships. What ever Talean said about me must be backed up by my appearance" he told himself while still looking into the mirror. I think I looked alright. He turned round on the mirror to look at his back. He rearranged his trousers and tightened his belt. He flushed the toilet, then opened the door and went to sit down behind the typewriter. Talean was on the phone again. Eddie made himself busy typing a letter for Talean. "You alright?" She asked, standing behind him. Her right hand was on his shoulder. The phone rang again; she turned round and took the receiver. After a brief conversation, she put down the receiver. "My visitor was on her way upstairs, she told Eddie. The door opened and in came the young lady.

The young lady came in with broad smiles. Eddie got up looked at her. She smiled again and looked at Ms Talean. Ms Talean got up, shook Shona's hand. "This is Eddie; he is a student at the University. He and I do the same course. He looked sexy and very athletic" she told Shona. Eddie stretched his hand for a hand shake with Shona. Her hand was soft and irresistible. A feeling went through his mind that he could not explain to himself. What a beautiful woman she was he said to himself. He received another big smile from her as she said in soft words" I liked your hair style. "That was very kind of you, thanks" Eddie said to her. Talean screwed her eyes at Eddie. "I have blown a gaff" he said to himself. I should not have said that. Talean looked a bit upset, but hid her feelings, turn round and beckoned to Eddie to follow. They walked down the stairs into the hall.

Miss, Miss, shouted Shady sitting on the carpet near the window. Her hand was up and bouncing up and down on the carpet. Talean and Eddie turned towards the kitchen. She turned round, looked at the child. Shady then asked "Who was this man?"

"Oh, I am sorry children, his name was Eddie. He came to see what we were doing in here. He came from Africa. Would you say hello to him kids.

A thunderous hello echoed the room, as Eddie and Talean walked up to the kitchen in silence. Ms Milam was washing up the kitchen trays and cleaning the kitchen tables. Eddie and Talean walked up to the stairs. They returned to the office in silence. Talean sat behind her desk. Eddie sat by the typewriter again. The phone rang. She took it and talked on the receiver. Eddie pretended to be reading a document lying idle right before him. "Could you ring back later" he heard her say before she put the receiver. He looked at her and smiled,

But Talean did not respond.

"You like Shona?" she asked Eddie. "She was beautiful you know, and single. Every man wants to talk to her.

"But you were more beautiful than her and you looked more elegant and gingerly than she was" he replied.

"Really?" She replied, smiling. Did you mean it or you just say it to make me feel good she said in a low conceding voice.

Eddie turned round to face Talean. "Look Talean I meant every word I say." He was now looking straight into her eyes. "It's all from the bottom of my heart." He said in a forceful voice.

Talean readjusted her self in her chair. "Alright, we were friends again. You could have her, you know, but not in this building. She finished her sentence with a loud bang on the table with her fist.

Eddie was a bit scared and knew that something was boiling in her mind.

"Look Talean, I came here to keep your company only, and nothing else. There was no point you introducing me to another woman.

"You better be, otherwise you would be in trouble. I tell you now. I am being serious about it." She told him

"I knew you being serious. I did see your facial expression" he told her.

She got up angrily walked up to the window, looked out briefly and then turned round to look at him.

Eddie sat like a good boy, with his hands fold on his laps. She came close to him, looked into his eyes,

"You were going to make a pass word if I had given you the chance. Anyway, did you like my office?

You have not said anything about my office. I thought it's a nice little room. The only problem at the moment was that every thing seemed to be every where, making it looked more like a store than an office."

She moved one pile of documents from the table and put it on the floor behind her chair to create more space on her desk.

Eddie smiled. "Yea man, your office was cozy and Commodious." Talean smiled and twisted her body in a happy and content fashion." You didn't mean that do you? Look how cramped this place was. It looked disgusting to me and showed that the person who worked in here was disorderly. I am not that disorderly. Some of these files have been lying here for years without anyone looking at them." She sat down and looked at Eddie.

Eddie looked round first and then at Talean. "I think what you needed was a system of filing, to sort out all these masses into subjects for easy reference.

Talean sat up and relaxed into her chair. You were right; I sometimes spent ages looking for a document for reference. Sometimes I did not even border myself, looking, I just write things on top of my head" she said casually.

Eddie relaxed into his chair, then moved it close to the table and rested his hands on the table. "I might be able to help you sort these out into files and make more room for you. That would make this place looked more like an office than it was now," he said in a relaxed voice.

Talean looked excited, as her face brightened up and full of smiles." You were a good man, you are a God send. I will …" She stretched her hands across the table, but hesitated, and withdrew them. She put her right hand into her open mouth. Reading the anguish in her face, Eddie stretched his hands across the table, as if he wanted to take the pen close to her hand. He played with the pen, looked at her "you alright?"

"Yes" she replied softly. "I wanted to touch your hands; I wanted to play with them, could I?" She asked in a fading voice. Without saying a word, but a smile that carried the message, he opened his arms which were now close together and almost touching hers. She brought hers slowly and hesitatingly at first and then clasped Eddie's palms. She moved her right palm up Eddies arm. He could feel the tenseness in her hand and the shaking of the hand too. The shaking got stronger and stronger. In silence they looked at each other. Eddie could see the burning passion in her eyes as they sink slowly into their sockets. She withdrew her hands quickly and covered her mouth. She sank back into her chair and moved her eyes slowly away from Eddie up to the ceiling. She was breathing very hard and deeply.

Eddie still had his hands across the table. "What was the matter?" he asked.

Her hands were still over her mouth. "No, nothing" she replied in a frightful voice. "I have been carried away. I am sorry," she said. "I didn't mean to. She pushed her chair back, as the door opened and a child came in with a pencil and a drawing book. Talean looked at the child with a cool eye, and her mouth folded into a nut. "Did you knock at the door?" she asked calmly.

"No Miss," he replied. "Then go out and knock at the door again. The child walked out, closed the door, and then knocked twice.

"Come in" she shouted. The boy came in again. "Good boy" she said. "What happened?' she asked.

"Miss told me to come up here because I could not go to sleep.

"Oh, oh every one was sleeping and you were trying to keep them awake?" He nodded his head.

"Eddie, could you give him that chair over there. You come and sit right by me, take that chair

Eddie moved the chair close to Talean, he then moved to the typewriter table. "Could I do some typing Miss?" he asked.

"Can you type and well too? "She asked, and Eddie nodded his head.

"Oh well, you would be typing my letters from now on. I did type but one character at a time and it took long to do a whole letter. I did have a letter actually that needed to be typed. Could you type it for me please" she said to him.

"Off course, I would type it with pleasure." he replied. He got up to get the letter.

"Thank you. You never say no, I love you for that. She smiled. He took the letter, returned to the typewriter. As Eddie typed the letter, she got up from her chair and come over to read the letter on the type writer. She stood behind Eddie, looked round to make sure that the child was not looking. She bent over Eddie, rested her breasts on Eddie's shoulder. She looked round again at the child. The child was looking at his drawing book. Eddie lifted his head up, as she lowered her face. The child called out "Miss" She hesitated and jacked herself up quickly. She turned round and noticed that the child was looking. She went over to him "What did you want? Oh ho, that was a good drawing you have made" she told the boy. "Who was this person? She asked. "This was my mum, and this was my dad. They were having their dinner." he replied proudly.

That was very good, you have done very well. Now you need to color the drawings alright. You take those crayons and color them neatly for me.

Eddie completed the letter. He got up to hand over the letter to her. She beckoned to him to put it on the table.

"Come let me show you the other room. They moved out and entered the other room with a large window and a suite of chairs by the window, tag boards and a side door slightly ajar. "This was our store room.. She opened the door. A tiny cubicle packed full with stationary, food and equipment. She looked through the window. "You could watch what was going on outside on the street from this window. Eddie leaned over the sofa to have a good look down the street. She leaned directly behind Eddie, pressing her breast on his back. As he turned his face round, he was directly in her arms. Eddie's heart was beating fast, as a shock wave of passion ran down his body. She sank into the settee, as she slowly knelt between his legs, caressing his legs. He lowered his head slowly. His lips touched hers. She opened her mouth to receive his tongue when the door racked open. The child came in. "I have finished coloring Miss" he said in a happy voice. She took the book off him, looked at it carefully. "That was very good. Could you now go down and lie quietly and go to sleep like all the other children. "Yes Miss" he replied.

Alright, quietly you go and do not say one word. I am coming down in a minute to see if you were sleeping. As the boy walked out in silence, she raised her head and closed her eyes for a moment. These children were behind your backside every minute of the day. Come let us go into my room. She pulled Eddie from the settee with her right hand. They walked back to the office in silence. She let Eddie in first, and without letting his hand go. She closed the door, leaning on it, as she raised Eddie's hand high up and threw it behind her. He sank into her arms. She held him tight, as she wrapped her arms round his body. They had a wet kiss and caressing each other. It went on as if it will not come to an end. They had foot steps on the stair case. The romantic session came to an abrupt end when she pushed him quickly; turn round to open the filing cabinet by the door. She pulled a document hurriedly and pretending to read it to Eddie. They both bend over the document as the door opened. Sharon. You read it, while I talk to sharon. She passed the long letter to Eddie. "Eddie was going to help us sort these documents lying all over this place. She spread her arms around the room. Eddie was still trying to make sense of the document handed to him. His mind was still filled with the memories of the kiss he just had. This was the tenderest kiss I have ever had, and probably the last. But no it's just the beginning . We are still in the first week of the term. We have one year long togetherness up to the end of the course.

"Have you read the letter through?" Talean asked, or you were still reading it, and thinking about its contents?" May be you were thinking about your college work. Would you come downstairs if you did not mind; Faye was going out and it's my turn to look after the kids.

Eddie turned round, the letter still in his right hand, his eyes met with Sharon's. She smiled and turned round to look at Ms Talean who was moving some documents from her desk. She dropped the documents besides the table on the floor. "Put back the documents in the draw, we were going down stairs. Some one needed her break. Sharon turned round, opened the door and walked out. Eddie had a quick glance at Talean, and then followed. Her face was full of smiles as always. She folded her lips into a nut, then threw a kiss at Eddie, as he made his way through the door. He smiled in return, and then walked out of the door, still smiling. Sharon looked at him, and then smiled back. She walked down a few steps then looked back at Eddie, smiled again.

"It's been a busy day, you know" she told Eddie. "I have not had a single quiet moment yet. When I got home in the evening, I felt so exhausted that sometime,

I could not eat my supper. I went straight to bed after a cup of tea. My aunt sometimes had to force me to eat.. Some other time, I just dosed off in the settee, as we watched the TV. Did you feel that exhausted some days?"

Eddie sat next to her on the chair. The children were sleeping except one who had woken up and was playing with a toy. He looked at her. "We all got exhausted sometime after a hard days work. I did get really tired sometime. There were times when I got so tired that I could not make myself an evening meal.

As Talean beckoned to Sharon to sit down, she was walking to wards the front door, she looked round, smiled and opened the door, walked out in silence. Talean got up walked to the kitchen to fetch a chair. She put it close to her, beckoned to Eddie to move to the chair by her. "It's quiet and peaceful" she whispered to Eddie. They had one hour rest each afternoon, about the same time.

CHAPTER 16

▼

Eddie sat quietly, reading the news paper. He turned the pages quickly. He then took the book, riled the pages to the end of the book.

What do we have tomorrow" Talean asked.

"I would be presenting my paper. Jady would be presenting hers too." He replied.

"Oh, I remember now. That should be very interesting indeed How great it is to sit down and listen to the first presentations, then discussed your paper and make suggestions. Oh what a day lovely day that is. It would be real fun. I have read your paper. Its good, very detailed. You should be getting an "A" grade for that paper, I bet you" She said in a confident voice.

Well, I am not sure about that, he replied in a calm voice. "Do not be optimistic, you get what I mean. It was going to be white against black. We make up the majority, but the lecturers were all white. He might not see things as we did. You wait and see.

It was ten O'clock, all the students were seated. Pocket conversations were going on.

The Professor walked in quietly "Good morning ladies and gentlemen" he said as he walked to the center of the room and stopped. The class answered in a chorus He looked around for a second, then walked on to his desk, put his file down and made a second look round again more slowly this time as if he was counting the number of students and then he sat down. "I have looked through the presentations for today. A lot of effort and hard work had been put into each essay. We will listen to the lady first, then Eddie. Thelma, you come first. Feel free to ask questions or make contributions to the discussion. The essence of this exercise was to supplement your reading, look at the points of view of other students on certain aspects of the course. Remember that you all would be making a presentation exercise as part of the course and grading process." The professor sat down.

It was Eddie's turn to present his essay. He got up walked to the desk next to the Professor. He sat down, then got up and read his essay at a moderate speed. He took questions which he answered with ease. The discussion went well. Students thought the essay was well written, with lots of information and precise details on various aspects in teacher accountability.

"The essay should earn Eddie an "A" grade" shouted one student from the back. This was followed by a chorus of "Yea"

The Professor sat motionless, with both hands over his mouth. He said nothing until the noise did down.

"It's your turn Ashley" he said, as he opened the other essay. Ashley got up, took her essay and walked to the desk. Eddie had now gone back to his seat. He sat down after receiving a big smile from Talean and head nods from his friends. She got up and read her essay quickly. It took less then ten minutes reading time which was far less than the recommended time. She took some questions, giving scant details in her answers, an indication of less knowledge of the subject matter.

"This essay was brief and lacking in details" Hansu pointed out. He then asked a question. One question followed another on the issues she raised on her essay. Some of her explanations were very brief and not very accurate. Some of the questions had to be answered by the professor, because she did not know the answer or she refused to answer the questions due to the fact that she raised many issues in her essay but she did not give answers or explanations on those issues. She looked very upset and frustrated, because she was overwhelmed by questions and criticisms. She got so upset that she refused to answer any more questions.

The Professor had to step in and took over the discussion and then answered the rest of the questions. She got up and left the table and walked angrily to her set. The professor got up and gave a short lecture on the topic to fill in the gaps. It was a timely intervention, as the atmosphere was getting polarized. All the white students thought her essay was good enough and the black students who make the majority thought it was too scanty and lacking in details and very brief and too shallow and not good enough information on the topic

The professor stood silent for a few second until every one was quiet "You should know that essays are written according to a persons back ground information, and his or her back ground information on the subject matter. I must confirm that both essays are good and provided lots of information on the topics.

The purpose of the exercise was not to judge who did better and who did poorly. We are here to learn from each other and provided information on what we already know and share that information with others.. We are not here to run a rat race. We have to congratulate each other for their effort; criticisms of a student's work and ideas had no place in the course the Professor said in a commanding voice. They should be replaced by commendations for each other's efforts.

One white female student got up and asked the Professor what grades he gave for the two essays.

He said Eddie had a "B" grade and Ashley had an "A" grade. There was an up roar of discontent amongst the students. The same student who got up and asked for the grades said "But we all gave Eddie an "A" grade for his essay. That was what he deserved for that essay." She said in a calm voice. "Yea" all the students replied.

"I have the final say" said the professor in an angry voice. The grade I have given was final. He got up took his folder looked round with an upset face "That was a good enough grade for him" he said as he walked out with angry quick steps.

Ada, a West Indian lady got up. "This was England. If you were white, you got a good grade for any quality of work you submit. You get what I mean? God have mercy on us. We are seen as renegade students. A "B~" grade was a very good grade for us, but Babylon deserved a better grade for less than minimum effort."

The white students all left as soon as the lecturer left the hall.

Eddie and Talean got up and followed. They walked to the lift in silence. Eddie was watching the counter above the lift when John a white student tapped his shoulder. He looked round, smiled. "That was a very good essay. You did very well. But that was also life, you just wanted to graduate. It was hard to swallow, but you just have to accept your fate. The lift came, and they all rushed in.

It was Wednesday evening. Talean came prepared to rehearse her essay for the next day. Eddie sat on the bed. She stood a few feet away from him, reading the essay. Eddie had researched it and written it in full for her.

She had copied it neatly in her own hand writing. Eddie listened carefully as she read in a moderate speed.

She made lots of mistakes in reading the essay for the first time and hardly understood the meanings of some of the words. Eddie had the original copy in his own hand writing. He stopped her now and again to explain the difficult words. She read the essay a second time to attain fluency. "I have read it three time over at home you know" she told him That was very good but you still have to read it a few more times so that it becomes yours at the presentation. He then asked her a few questions she would expect. He went through the answers with her. He handed to her the written answers to the questions he was asking.

The rehearsal went on for an hour and a half, until she was confident of what she was doing. "I would answer any question asked, that you did not know the answer" he assured her.

"Oh, Eddie, you did not know how nervous I am. I did not know what I am doing. You wrote this essay, you knew exactly what it was, and you would be able to answer any questions with ease on this essay. I honestly have no idea. I have read the book, the articles in the research papers and journals, but I did not understand what they were saying" she said in a subservient voice. She pulled her chair forward close to the bed. "I have to read it ten more times to understand it and be able to answer question on it, honest."

Eddie relaxed in the bed. He lay on his back, both hands behind his head on the pillow. "Do not worry about the question. You simply needed to take your time and read the essay carefully and clearly. I would answer the questions for you."

It was Thursday morning. Eddie got up early, looked round. He walked to the window, to look outside. The weather was nice, with blue skies and he opened the window. The early morning cool and gentle breeze was blowing into the room. He walked to the bathroom to brush his teeth and took his usual morning shower.

The kitchen was quiet when he got there. He boiled an egg quickly before the lot came in. He made his tea in a hurry and walked back to the dinning hall.

Eddie left for the University in a hurry to meet Talean. He wanted to get there before her. She was already there in the foyer waiting for him. He opened the first glass doors and then the second glass doors and saw Talean on the bench sitting anxiously. As Eddie entered the foyer, she got up, went forward to meet him. Eddie could see the signs of anxiety on her face. He smiled. "I thought I was going to get here before you he told her.

"Oh Eddie "she said in a soft voice. "I got up very early this morning. I did not even have breakfast. I wanted to catch the second bus to Birmingham. Luckily, I did not have long to wait. I got the express bus from town to here. They went up the three steps to the lift. "Oh Eddie, I am very nervous about the presentation" she said as she put both hands on her breast. I am not too sure how this exercise would go, honest."

Eddie was looking at the counter above the lift. "You should not be worried about it. He would have given you a grade already on what you presented to him. This was an exercise we all have to go through, so do not even think about it. I would not, honest. Besides, I am there to prop you up.

Eddie came out of the lift first, followed by Talean. They walked into the lecture room. Lots of the students were already there. Talean looked round. "There were two seats over there" she pointed to the seats in the far corner. They walked across the lecture room and sat down. The students were talking to themselves in small pockets. The humming sound of everyone talking together could be heard. Eddie and Talean sat quietly for a while. Talean opened her file. Her heart was beating like a little tom tom. She took Eddie's left hand, whispered into his ear, "you wanted to feel my heart beat, put your hand under my breast. It's beating violently.

"Calm down and just relax;" he told her in a dismissive voice.

The door opened, and the class went silent. The Professor walked to his desk. He sat down, looked round, and then took out his attendance register. He looked through it, and then counted the number of students in class.

"This was the third set of presentations' he said. "These were discussion classes which I thought were good for you. It was not always for you to come and listen to us all the time. We designed these discussions on the premise that you get a better understanding of a topic through discussions. Secondly the course was too intensive; we could not fit in all the topics in lecture time. The discussions were so far going very well.. The next set of discussions will be given out next week. This masters program was designed to enable students to research a good portions of the program . That would enable you to develop reading habits and widen your horizons on the subject. Those who survived these exercises were the very good students at the end of the day. We better get down to business. Today we have two presentations as usual, Talean and Matthew. Get yourselves ready while I do the attendance."

"We would start with Talean "he announced. She got up walked to the desk, and sat down. Her face was tense. She looked at Eddie who was not even watching her

The time went fast. She was sweating. She had a kerchief besides her. By conscientious, her essay was thought to be good enough.

"Why would you not let her answer the questions herself Eddie?" asked Linda at the back seat.

Eddie got up, smiled and put his hands on the desk for support. I was not out of place, we worked together,

Besides that, if you know the answer to a question, you could answer it in her place. It's your own contribution to the discussion I think. The Professor told us that we should read about the topic and made contributions during the discussion where you could."

The Professor, who sat in a reclined position, nodded his head in approval.

Talean answered the last question from Moses. She had the answer written on the paper Eddie gave her. She had time to look through it while Eddie was talking. She got up put her hand on her breast as she walked back to her seat. There was a big applause, as she tiptoed to her seat. She had a big smile of content on her face. Eddie welcomed her with a broad smile. She breathed a heavy sigh of relief

It was Matthew's turn to present his essay. He walked to the desk, sat down, and then got up to read his essay. He sat down, and a flood of questions followed. He answered some of them. But even those he answered, some of the answers were inadequate. Sometimes the answers were ambiguous and not to the point. No one made any hard comment for fear of victimization by the Professor.

The professor asked what the students thought about the second paper. Surprisingly, no one said a word for a while. Then one white student at the back said the essay was alright. The student then asked "What grades have been given for these two essays?"

The professor refused to tell the students but they got to know that Talean got a "C+" grade and Matthew got a "B" grade

In the last presentations, one student asked the Professor "why do black students get fewer grades for better essay then the white students? The Professor was busy looking at his folder. One West Indian student said" This is England" The professor lifted his eyes without lifting his head to see who was talking.

The professor told the class that there will be another round of this exercise, but the next round will be with Dr. Judith on the 7th floor in the main lecture room. He got up and walked out of the room

CHAPTER 17

▼

Eddie was spending a day at the Marcus Garvey Day Care center and he was looking after the kids as they took their afternoon nap.

The atmosphere was quiet and peaceful. The noise seeping in was that of people passing and speeding cars along the street. Eddie occasionally looked through the window and sometime at a car zooming up the street. Sometimes people walk on either side of the road, stop briefly and look into the nursery. He could see people coming into the corner shop, opposite the day care center. He sat quietly watching the little kids sleeping on foam mattress. Some of the children had their clothes on, others didn't. Those without clothes on must be bed wetting lot while they slept Eddie thought. He could hear the sound of the washing machine coming from the kitchen. He remembered that he had seen a small washing machine. Some kids did get accidents during the day time while in the day care center; some came in with dirty clothes that needed to be cleaned. The washer went on most of the day each day.

Eddie glanced at the clock on the wall directly opposite his chair. It was ticking towards 1.45 pm. We would Wake the children up at 2pm Talean told him. They would go outside to play for one hour before the parents started arriving in the center to pick their kids up. Eddie was looking through the window when the front door opened. The three girls walked in, One of then girls shoes made audible noise, the boy who was playing quietly lifted his head; he looked round; and then raised his hands and feet attracting attention. Talean hushed him up, by putting her right index finger over her lips.

"Back to sleep now, you dare get up or make noise" shouted Faye.

The ladies walked to the coat rack, hung their coats. They winged their eyes at each other and smiled. "He was still here" whispered Jennifer.

"Hi, Eddie, you were enjoying some peace and quiet?" asked Faye. "This was the only time we have real rest" she said as she walked to the large front window with a large colored drawing of a child.

"You lot could get up now and get your clothes. I would do some and you do the rest" Faye told Jennifer. One by one the children got up, took their clothes and joined the line by Faye waiting to be dressed. She helped one child after another dressed up. She was soon surrounded by all the children, some naked, others half naked. Joyce took one child. The child walked on her toes. "She had an accident while sleeping and wet her self. Talean was busy tiding the foam mattresses into a single pile. She took the pile from the floor, stole a glance at Eddie before walking quickly into the kitchen to put them in the store room.

Eddie smiled back as she walked away. She came back knelt down to help dress the children. As each child was dressed up he or she ran quickly across the hall to the toilet door and join the queue. Two queues have been formed outside the door as each child waited for his turn to use the toilet before running outside to play. Talean went into the toilet to help Joyce. The children came out of the toilet, and then ran outside quickly shouting through the back door into the garden with toys, slides, bikes and trampoline. As the last child ran out, Joyce and Talean followed them into the play ground. Eddie got up and went outside with the rest of the staff. The play ground was a small house back yard with a big pear tree. It was half paved with cement, not quite suitable for very young children's play ground.

Eddie stood by the window over looking the playground. One boy about four years old, came to Eddie with a bike "push me" he told Eddie. Joyce said to Eddie, "he wanted you to push him around."

Eddie bent over to push the child on the tricycle. Talean who was receiving kids at the base of the slide said "Oh, oh, you have got a friend already. That was very good. They won't let you stand by idly, while they need someone to push them around. The next minute Eddie was surrounded by three girls. They looked at him with amazement; one of them said "What is your name"

"Eddie" he replied. "What is your name?" Eddie asked, looking at "Shady. She is Tina, and Michelle" she touched each girl in turn.

"Eddie" Shady replied. She came close to Eddie, stood before him. She turned round and had her back on his legs. She put her hands round his legs.

"Mr. Kamira" Talean said as she came to join the conversation. "Call him Mr. Kamira, alright children?"

"Yes Miss" they answered.

"Where did you come from?" asked Shady.

"Selly Oak" Eddie replied, playing with Shady.

Talean bent over to talk to the children. "He came from Africa" she told the children.

"Africa! Where was that?" Shady asked, looking at Talean. Her face showed some mixed emotion.

It's in selly Oak" shouted Tina into Michelle's face, then jumped up and down. "Don't be stupid, she told Michelle.

Talean shook her right hand. No, no Africa was not in Selly Oak.

"Where was it then? Tina asked quickly.

"It's a long way from here" she said in a soft voice.

"Was it far away like London was? I went to London with my mom. It's a long way from Birmingham.

"Africa was across the ocean. You have to go on an airplane to get there," she told the kids.

"Oh my dad did fly on the airplane to go to Ethiopia, you know. Shady said in a proud voice.

We went to the sea side in Black pool" Tina said.

Me and my mom went to Black pool the other day. There were lots of rides and lots of water there" Michelle said.

"Listen to me girls. Africa was a long, long way away. You have to cross the sea to get there. Black people lived there," she told them.

"Oh. Like Handsworth? Shady asked?

Without saying another word, Talean ran quickly to help a girl who fell off the swing.

"Africa—"and before Eddie could complete pronouncing the word, the girls ran off in opposite directions. The boy on the Bike ran and jumped on the trampoline.

Eddie walked towards the swing and stood by Talean. "How long do you have them out here for? He asked.

Talean was busy pushing the boy on the swing. And without looking at him she replied" one to two hours depending on when the parents picked them up. Parents started picking them up from the play ground at 3.00pm. We took them in at 3.45 pm and they either watch the telly or read a story to them. We could not keep them in doors for too long. They got bored, and some of them become mischievous.

Eddie took over pushing the boy on the swing, while Talean went to talk to a parent who stood by the side door with a boggy and two younger children. The girl who was older under three years of age hung on her mom's dress. The little boy about a year old sat on the boggy sleeping.

"Shady" a wave of shouting went across the play ground. "Your mom is here." Reluctantly Shady went down the two steps to the pavement floor. Upset and in a crying mode she went to her mom. "You don't want to go home? Talean said to Shady as she held the girl's hand and looked into her face.

Shady shook her head no, and her body left to right. "I want to play" she said in a crying voice. Her mom looked up into the sky, as she closed her eyes. If you wasted my time, I would smack your bottom" her mother shouted in a menacing voice. "Pass mek we go now." Reluctantly the girl walked pass Talean, as her mom wheeled round the boggy. "Me see you tomorrow" she told Talean, as she pushed the boggy with one hand and push Shady with the other hand to make her walk fast.

They walked into the hall, then through the front door Talean turned to Eddie "You see what I mean, the children were happier here. They have free place to play. Before she completed the statement, another child was screaming, as his mom dragged him pass the door.

"You wouldn't believe it, some of the children run and hide as their mom came in to pick them up.

"Why was that? Eddie asked. "Children often like to go home with their parents.

"Well, it's a long story. The parents beat them at home. They did not allow them to play, and some children have no where to play at all. They just sit them down to watch the telly all the time. They even went out for a walk, go shopping or go to the pub and leave them alone in the house. A lot of these children were abused at home.

"How did you know that they were abused at home? Eddie asked.

Without answering, she led the way, saying come lets go up to the office. They walked through the back door into the hall. They went up the stairs. Did you know that all our moms were single parents, and most of them were unemployed and have very little or no education at all. Talean flung on her chair, as she breath a sigh pf relief out of exhaustion. "I am exhausted. You see what we did each day. In fact, that was just part of what we did each and every day.

Were you exhausted yourself?" she asked. Eddie nodded. She pulled him and gave him a long kiss which Eddie thought would never come to an end. She pulled her mouth away, smiled and gave him another quick peck. "I felt better now" she said in a low and deep voice. "I needed this you know after a long and hard days work. Didn't you yourself?

Eddie nodded three times. "You have sweet and tender lips you know" he told her.

Talean shrug off her shoulder in contempt. She smiled looked at him. "Do I?" she asked.

"Yes for sure "he replied in a sharp tone. He nodded repeatedly.

She turned the chair quickly. Eddie turned round to look through the window. They both looked down into the play ground, as they heard foot steps coming up the stairs. She quickly turn her chair round and moved it to her desk, took a pen and was writing into her note book as the door opened.

CHAPTER 18

▼

Talean was still busy writing notes into her note book. Eddie was looking out through the window into the back yard. The pear tree had some fruits on it; some were big and ready for harvest. Eddie thought of how he could reach those big and delicious green pears up the tree. And in came a young lady with shoulder length hair, a gray blouse and long black skirt. She was in her thirties. Her hair was tied to a pony tail nut. She had a blue scarf round her neck. Her spongy lips were covered in red lip stick.

She was slightly out of breath as she stepped into the room, putting her head in first before she came in. She tiptoed up to the front of the desk, stood in silent before Ms Talean, with her hands crossed before her laps.

Ms Talean appeared very busy writing into her note book.

Eddie too was busy looking down the play ground as the children run around the playground. He watched the children running around, some climbing on the little cherry tree close to the boundary wall. He looked round and was greeted by broad smile. But he remained passive and motionless. He had a good feeling inside him. "This broad smile was not only entertaining but inviting as well "he told himself. But he decided to do or say nothing. How could Talean receive this if she saw me return this smile, or say something to this young lady? It was obvious that Eddie was accepted and welcomed, because a woman only smiled to a man if she accepts him, otherwise she would frown. Besides the body language was clear and the gestures were all clear and pointing to only one thing. I am on the right track" he told himself.

"Excuse me Miss" she said in a soft and polite voice. Talean looked up slowly, as she dropped her pen.

"Oh sorry, Sharon, I was just jotting down some of the things I would be doing tomorrow.

"Miss Vaughn was down stairs, she wanted to talk to you but she said she had Arthritis and she could not climb the stairs up to here.

"That was very nice of you. You could have buzzed me up instead of you coming up here. Well, I tell you what it's very respectful of you to come up and tell me. Thank you. I appreciated your effort. I am taking my bag and coat downstairs so that I would not have to come up here again later. I am on early tomorrow.

"Oh oh, I see your point now. You would soon be in peace. Who was on late today?

Talean pulled her face back. "I think it's you Miss" Jennifer said in a low voice.

"It's me?" Talean put her right hand on her chest. I never knew that its my turn to stay here until all them kids are gone home. Oh God, have mercy on me.

Talean had mixed feelings. Eddie would stay with her if she was going to stay till late. But she was not sure if he would like to stay that late in the daycare center. She has to take him to the bus stop and see him on the bus to the city center. But she could not do that if she had to look after the late kids. She bent her head down as she walked away towards the window, looked out of the window and came back to her seat.

Jennifer walked out, closed the door behind her without saying another word.

Talean got up and walked to Eddie who was listening but appeared to be looking through the window, and enjoying the scenery in the garden.

"It's a lovely scene watching the kids playing in the garden. They move ever so fast from one activity to another.

"Yea man, the children were very happy when they come into the day care center. She walked back to her desk, took her hand bag, opened it and took out a small mirror and lip stick. "I would be down there for the rest of the afternoon" she said while painting her lips with the lip stick. "Are you staying with me until we break off? I will not be able to see you off at the bus stop before all the kids are gone. I would take you to Soho Road to see on your bus, because I would not like you to take the bus in the opposite direction"

Eddie walked back to his seat. "I would wait if you wanted me to" he said in a calm voice.

That was good, I would make you some food before you leave" she said in a contended voice. She packed her bag, swing it round her left shoulder. She then balanced herself on her right leg, took three step towards Eddie, bent over, touch his lips with her right index finger. She looked straight into his eyes. She folded her lips inwards, then she said get up and lets go down stairs. She turned round and led the way out. As she walked majestically down the stairs, Eddie was behind her.

"What message was she conveying?" he thought. I do not know a thing what she was on about. But it seemed that Eddie was acceptable and welcome. The body language and gestures were clear, he thought.

"I am on the right track" he assured himself. The idea came to his mind to ask her why she touched his lips.

No, I will not ask he convinced himself. I will let sleeping dogs lie.

Talean stopped at the first landing, turned round to look at Eddie. He stopped suddenly; she was only inches away from him. Her begging eyes were saying something which Eddie missed out all together. She smiled, turned round and walked on. She doubled her steps, and got to the hall while Eddie was half way down the stairs. "Lazy man" she said jokingly with a broad smile. "You should be running down these stairs. We keep fit going up and down these stairs all day each day."

"Oh gush, it's a bit tiring going up these stairs" he exclaimed. He turned round to look at the stairs again.

The wooden stair case was winding and had stood the test of time; it was sometimes rocky, making noise as one went up or down them. Some boards have been changed over time but some were still there that have worn out and needed to be replaced.

"Sit on that chair" Talean told him, pointing to a chair near the large window.

"Thank you" he said as he sat down. He could not hear what she was saying to him. The children were running round, screaming and shouting.. She came up, "oh, oh" she clapped her hands, saying sit down now, all of you; fingers on your lips. "Chantelle, put your finger on your lips now" she said in a raised voice. "You could play without screaming and running around.

The front door opened, as a boggy was pushed in through it.

"Jadi your mum was here" all the children said in a chorus

She got up and ran across the hall to her mums hands.

"Good afternoon Miss Talean. Jadi raised her head from her mum's shoulder, looked round. She waved and said "bye children. Her mum turned round and walked out, dragging the boggy behind her.

Talean came and sat down near Eddie. She looked out through the window, then her watch. "We expected all these lot to be picked up by 5.30. But sometimes we had to take them home, or leave them with another Parent."

"Why would the parent not pick them up on time?" Eddie asked.

"Well, some work late, others go out and fail to come home on time. On one occasion, the parent was arrested in Stoke-on—Trent for shop lifting.

"You mean" he did not complete the sentence when Talean got up, took one kid and rushed her to the toilet.

She was shaking her head, as she carried the girl on her toes.

She came back and sat down, looked at Eddie. "You would not believe, but it happens quite often. Some of them could not pay the 0.50p a day for looking after the child, with break fast and one full meal and two snack breaks."

"Was that all they pay?" he asked. It seems too little he thought.

"That seemed too little, but you would not believe it, some could not afford to pay that money. There were parents who owed the center nearly one hundred pounds sterling in arears.

"That was not right; how come that these parents owed so much to the center and how did you pay your bills?

"Well, if the parents did not pay the fees, we could not throw out the kids from the center. That was the policy of the Harambee Organization, not to throw out any kid for not paying the fees. We could only send reminders to the parents for fees, but if they did not pay we had nothing to do about it.

"What about parents who paid regularly?" he asked.

Talean sat silent for a while then said in a moderate voice, "We congratulate them for their effort. That was all."

Talean put her index finger on her lips again to stop the kids talking. She got up to talk to a parent who had just come in. The parent left with her son. Talean walked back to her seat as the door closed behind her. "You see this lady going just out" she said. "She owed this center seventy eight pounds sterling. She was a single parent with five children and she was not working."

Eddie got up walked to the toilet, came back and sat down. There were now three children left to go. He sat down quietly looking at the kids who were talking with signs. Talean went into the kitchen to make dinner for Eddie. Eddie got up and followed her to the dinning hall where the kitchen is." I still did not understand what you were trying to say. Why do these women not go out to work?

"Eddie," she called out. "You would not believe it, but these women got more money than I do each week. They receive money each week for each of these children. So the more children they have the more money they got each week. **Besides that they got free housing for being unemployed. They were better than us who have no children and were working. She was illiterate, but she** believes that working for a white man is against their beliefs. They call the white man BABYLON. Me can work fe Babylon no way. They would tell you" She performed a little dance to demonstrate how they speak about Babylon.

The children laughed.

"Is it funny?" she asked them. One shook his head, the others said nothing, but had their hands over their mouth.

"I am talking about your parents children" she bowed down before them. "Your parents were lazy, and did not want to work."

"My mum works" said the boy. "She was a dinner lady at Wattville school.

"Oh yes, that was good, but not good enough." she replied.

"My mum went to college" said one of the girls. Talean got up. The door opened and another parent came in.

"Mitchelle, Talean called out. "Get your coat from the table. All the coats have been put on one table in the kitchen, ready for collection as the parents came in one after another. She told Eddie to keep an eye on the two kids while she went into the kitchen. She sat besides Eddie. "Are you alright?" she asked

Eddie nodded his head. "You liked a drink?" and without waiting for an answer she got up. "Keep an eye on these lots." She walked into the kitchen.

Eddie sat still for a while, and then got up to talk to the kids kicking at each other. He knelt before them, and spoke to them in whispers. Stop it he said in a quiet voice.

"He kicked me first, pointing to the boy sitting directly opposite him, with his thumb in his mouth.

"No, you kicked me first. He was sticking his tongue at me. He has been nasty to me." he replied.

"Then you kick him?" Eddie asked.

"No, he kicked me first."

Talean walked back slowly, with two drinks in glass cups on the tray. She handed the tea cup to Eddie.

"Are these lot mucking about?" she asked

Eddie was now getting up from his seat replied; "they were kicking at each other.

She took a seep of tea and put the cup beside her. "Come here both of you" she said. They came and stood side by side in front of her. "Take your finger off your mouth" she told Kevin. "Who started kicking first?"

The boys turned and looked at each other, and then they pointed a finger at each other. "He was being nasty to me," Kevin said. "No, you were nasty to me as well," pushing his face close to Kevin's. Kevin pushed his face away and smacked him on the face. Talean grabbed both of them and pulled them away. Talean looked at Kevin in the eye. "Well," she said "Why did you smack him?" She shook him. Kevin burst into tears. She dragged him to the corner of the room and sat him down on the carpet his face towards the wall and walked back quickly.

"She looked at George with a stern eye. "You better behave" she said to him. She looked at him again in the eye. "Not one more word, sit there and your face turned to the wall."

Breathing a sigh of relief, she turned to Eddie. "You see what we went through each day. You would never have a moment of peace. You keep a constant vigil, on these lot." She took a sip of her tea. Is your tea alright? she asked turning round to Eddie.

"It's a lovely cup of tea, honest, the sugar is just right." he replied with smiles.

"I was not too sure how much sugar you needed, and I did not want to ask you.. I just guessed it."

"You guessed it right. That was excellent" he said in a deep voice.

She put her hand on her chest and bent forward slightly. "I have done one thing right today" she said smiling. He smiled in response to her gesture.

"Miss" George called out pointing to a mum standing by the door. Her son sat in the far corner with his face to the wall. Talean got up, told Kevin to get his coat. She then walked to the door, opened it. Hello, Tilly, I did not see you coming. She had a long black winter coat. She walked in. "He was being naughty?" she asked

"He was mucking about with that boy sitting by the window. George had now turned round to see who came in. "Kevin come your mum is here. Angry with a twisted face he walked quickly to his mum, flung himself into his mum's hands and burst into tears. "Just stop crying" she told him in an angry voice. One more time you get this one" she raised her right hand" on your bottom". "You have been naughty, I told you to behave, while you were in the nursery, didn't I?" Kevin's mouth still flattened with intermittent subs, he nodded yes. She pushed him forward. "Go on" she said..

She turned round to Talean "Thank you miss, I would see you tomorrow.

He has been a good boy all day, just this last minute. Children act silly sometimes. It's just one of them things. He knew that if he behaved in the nursery he would have sweets when he got home. If not his bottom would go sour and no sweets. Kevin burst into loud cry as his mum dragged him out of the door..

"He spoiled his evening" Eddie remarked. "He would get a good beating either on the way home or at home."

"I am sure about that "Talean added.

Eddie looked at his watch.

You wanted to go home now? She asked

"No, I just wanted to know what time it was." He told her.

"You have a good watch on; let me have a good look at it.

He pushed his hand close to her lap. She held it, put it on her lap> twisting and turning it slowly.

"Was it gold plated?" She asked.

"Well, I am nor too sure but it's a bit expensive" he told her.

She let go his hand, as she heard the door squawked open. A mum came in. She got up walked to the kitchen, put the cups in the sink, went to the table to get George's coat. "George, your mum was here. The child ran across in front of her to his mum. As Talean emerged from the kitchen, with George's coat in her left hand she said "we were almost there" The last two parents were coming in she said, without looking round.

"Isaack and Natalie get your coats; your mums were coming in. The children got up, ran to the table as the door opened. "Are we late,?" one parent asked. All the children were gone already. Sorry if we were late" she said.

"Not really" Talean replied. "Sometimes we had parents coming in early to pick their children. It just happened that you are the last one to come in today. Its just 4.30 "she added. I should go home early today.

I see you tomorrow" Talean said to them.

The lady in dark green dress and slightly ruffled hair and black high hill shoes cleared her throat. She was in her thirties, and carried two heavy shopping bags in both hands. She turned round and led the way out. The children said bye Miss together and walked out. As the door closed behind them, Talean turned to Eddie, looked straight into his eyes. "Well, we have this whole building to ourselves. It's nice to have a moment of peace and quiet. I tell you what; this was an odd day in the week. There were times when we have kids here up to 6.30. I am really surprised that they were all gone so early. She got up walked to the window, looked out on the street and came back. She sat down, and then pulled her chair close to Eddie. She took both his hands, saying "tell me what you wanted us to do now. I have something in mind," without waiting for Eddie to say something. She Squeezed his hands together, brought them to her cheeks, as she moved her head forward. "Cook, eat and take you to the bus stop or what?" There was a moment's silence. She adjusted her weight on the chair, pulled her gray skirt down to her knees, and then adjusted her white blouse. She slapped Eddie's thigh saying "stop looking at my breast, naughty man. You were not going to get it now, so do not get worked up. Do not even think about it." She looked into his eyes with her mouth folded inwards and tight lips.

With a smile Eddie said "I have no ideas, what ever you decided would be great for me. You tell me what you have in mind. I am in your care. Anything you said would be fine by me." he said to her

"Well, there was some food in the kitchen. I would warm it up; we would eat it, and then walk with you to the bus stop. I would see you on your bus, then I would catch my bus home. She let go his hand; got up, and then bend over him. She put both hands on his cheeks, shook his head gently. She lifted his head and looked into his eyes, closed her own eyes and gave him a gentle kiss. She walked towards the kitchen, then beckoned to Eddie to follow her. He got up and followed her into the dinning area. He stopped half way, looked at the triangular little tables stacked neatly near the side window in fours. The little chairs were also stacked neatly into three piles near the window. "What type of dinner do you cook in the hostel, English, Jamaican or African? " She asked.

I cooked "African meals, sometimes a mixture of both. I am a good cook you know" he told her. He took an expert look at the food in a big Aluminum German pot. A mixture of brown rice, brown roasted chicken drumsticks. He moved closer, put his left hand on the pot handle to admire the color and smell. Talean was sorting out the cutlery in the tray next to the pot. She turn round, stood askance looking at him. She had a cooking spoon in her right hand. "You telling me that you can cook well, but not as good as a woman" she remarked.

"Better than a woman sometimes you know, he replied calmly.

Talean put the spoon in the pot, her face showed some surprised contours.. She walked quickly into the kitchen, came back with a box of matches to light the stove. "You were both a silly and awkward man. You despised women. You mean you could cook better than a woman."

Eddie took the pot across to the stove, as Talean adjusted the flame. He put it over the flame.

"Thank you" she said, without lifting her head. She lowered her head to inspect the flame.

Eddie moved away, and stood directly behind her. She stood up quickly, turned round to face him, with a neutral face. He smiled and remained motionless. She turned round again to look at the food, stirred it. She then turned the flame down. Her left hand still on the stove for support, then said "I would come and cook a dinner for you this Sunday. Could I?"

Eddie had moved back, his back was now against the table, with both hands behind his back Cushing his bottom. Talean came close, pressed her whole body against him. She slowly pressed her face on his.

She pushed her tongue into his mouth which he seized like a hungry dog; gobbling his dinner. He could feel a wave of heat transferring from her breast to his chest and thighs as he slowly closed his hands around her. She wriggled and moved away, she stood a few feet away from him. She lowered her head, and then slowly surveyed him from his belt line, where a small mound had developed. She slowly lifted her head to look at his face, and then put her index finger over her mouth as she looked into his eyes. She gazed at him standing askance with both hands on her hip. He smiled, while she frowned. "You couldn't, you know. I would not let you," she said. She moved to the stove, turn off the stove. "Give me two plates from that draw please" she told him pointing to the draw by his right hand. He held the draw handle and noticed that it was rusty brown and held only by a loose nut. He pushed the draw back and held it with both hands at the base and then pulled gently. Inside the draw was a mosaic of all sizes and length of cutlery; baby spoons, cooking and frying spoons, eating and cutting knives. "Did kids come in here to get spoons?" he asked.

"No" she replied, turning quickly to him. "Why?" she asked.

"The dinner smells good" he said. He took out a large long spoon, put it in the pot.

"Yes, we have a good cook. Mrs. Milam had been cooking our dinner all the time here before I came over here. We ate good food every day of the week.. "There you are," handing him a plate full of rice and pears, two drumsticks and cold slaw. Take a spoon or folk from the draw.

"Thank you" he said, as he received the food with both hands smiling. "this was the best day I have had for years" he said in a soft voice.

"You men you have not been in the company of a woman for ages. I would not believe that, you know." You men could not go without a woman for too long. Your system could not hold up for any length of time. We the women could live alone for an endless period of time. I really mean that."

"I enjoy your company, the food and every thing. Spending time away from books and the four walls in your room was quite nice. Having some one like you to talk to and to serve you was even greater.

She open her eyes and dilated her pupils, she said "you enjoyed my company. I love to hear that, honest. I thought I am a boring woman and unpleasant to talk with. You really enjoyed my company, for true?"

"Very much" he replied..

"You sure about that?" she said in an exciting voice

Eddie nodded twice.

Well, I have been told many times that I was boring and have nasty attitudes." She told him.

"Boring," he repeated. "Nothing like that, I found you very pleasant. I do, Honest. There were not many pleasant women around like you."

"Hmm. Thank you for telling me. I thought I always put off people, the way I talk."

"No, you didn't, in fact you draw people closer to you than you think," he told her. He ate his food slowly'

"I have not drawn you too close to me though?" she asked.

Eddie said nothing, he continued eating his dinner.

She poured orange juice drink for him. "You like rice and peace, don't you?"

"Yes, but I could not cook it." he told her.

"You mean you could not cook this Our National Dish. What could you cook then? I thought you were a good cook."

"You were eating at mine on Sunday. I would give you the best of my home dish." He assured her.

"Oh ho" she jumped with joy. My taste buds are already getting wet. I am looking forward to that, honest.

I do." She told him. She put her hands round his neck. "I would spend most of the day with you. We would discuss our work. But was your girl friend not coming to see you Sunday? I did not want to be beaten up at your place. I could fight though, especially stubborn men. "She folded her fist and stretch her arm. "You see this, it was for naughty men.

"I have no girl friend" he told her

"You sure about being single?" She asked in a loud tone.

"Positive" he replied

"Please explain how come that you have no girlfriend when every man had a girl friend.

Eddie got up took his plate with the spoon still in his hand.

"Well, it's a fact of life. He put the plate on the table. He scooped a spoonful, lifted it then put it back.

He walked to the sink to put the plate in the sin.

"Well, I would find out sooner or later. She turned round looked at Eddie. "Oh, no put it on the tray please. I would wash it. It's a woman's job. "You were a gentle and kind man. Most men would not come near a kitchen. You want to do what I should be doing.

Eddie stamped his foot. "Why would you not let me do this simple washing exercise?" I wanted to do something' he said. He held the dish cloth. I spend one hour in the kitchen each day.

"This is my kitchen, just relax" she said without lifting her head. May be he just wanted to be close to me she thought. "I am serving you. Its my pleasure to serve you. I would wash and dry them up. The kitchen was a woman's world, not a man's. You get that right? I am supposed to do that." She got up took the tray, emptied it in the bin.

Eddie relaxed on the chair, poured some water into the cup. "You were right actually. In Africa, a man could not come near a kitchen. It's a forbidden place for him. But here was different. In fact we have a tribe in the West of Sierra Leone where the men do the cooking and washing up most of the time.

Talean turned on the tap to wash the plates. "I would not be able to eat again when I got home. My Aunt would be upset for wasting her dinner.

"Neither me," he added. "In fact there was no cooked meal in the hostel. I would just get on to my books as soon as I got back to the hostel.

She threw a hand towel at him saying "wipe you hands and mouth."

"Thank you "he said.

Eddie moved to the front door. He looked through the glass window onto the street. The corner shop across the street was open with people coming and going.

Talean shut the window, hurried to check the back door. She took the keys from the keys box. "Give me a sec," she rushed to the toilet. She came out a few minutes later. "I would lock up turn the alarm on, and then we go."

They emerged from the front door. She bolted the door, turned round, swinging her blue stripped skirt.

Eddie looked at her for a second. "You dressed gorgeously. Your white blouse was a perfect match with your skirt. She stood still for a moment, surveyed herself from foot to her chest. In a surprised tone she said "were you being sarcastic or what? This was by no means the best of my dresses This attire was purely a working dress.

"No, I really meant what I said. You looked lovely. The colors were more distinct now that we were outside."

Thank you then. We needed to be praised for everything didn't we?" she asked with a giggle. With a nudge on his shoulder they moved. This day care center has been running for years, and nothing had been improved.

"But it looked alright to me." he said. He stopped looked back at the building from a distance.

They walked slowly on the side walk up the road to the bus stop at Soho road.

They got to the bus stop. "Join the queue" she told him. "The bus will soon be here"

"The bus is coming "shouted a child.

"This bus would take you to the city center, and then you catch number 61 or 63 to Selly Oak.

He turned round to her "are you not coming onto this bus?"

"No, I am going in the opposite direction. I catch my bus on the other side of the road. You take care I would see you tomorrow at the University.

"Thanks for everything" he said as he board the bus. Talean waited until the bus moved before she crossed the road to catch her bus.

Eddie came off the bus and walked quickly across the street and down the road. Suddenly and from no where Obusah appeared, walking along side Eddie.

"Oh man, where have you been? I have not seen you all day. I wanted to borrow your book on policy development. I thought you have been kidnapped today you know.

"Kidnapped" Eddie repeated. No man I went on a visit.

"A visit to a day care center already, where did you go for the visit?" Obusah asked

"At a day care center, somewhere in the city, I could not even tell you exactly where it was, honest" replied Eddie.

"You must be a great man to be invited to visit a center so soon." Obusah said in a deep voice.

"It was Talean actually who asked me to come over to the center.

"Hmm, you must have had a good day." Obusah said as he looked at Eddie with admiration.

"Oh yes, I met all the staff. I had dinner and stayed all day to observe how they ran the day center.

"You are a great man. Did you talk to the female staff? Were they friendly?" he enquired.

"Yes, very friendly indeed. The staff were all women, you would not believe it. It was a pleasant experience, I must admit."

"But you did not make any contact as yet?" Obusah asked

CHAPTER 19

▼

Eddie and Obusah went into the hostel together. Obusah was very curious to know what Eddie found out about the day center. He had a lot of questions for Eddie. He decided to follow Eddie into his room. Would you like to tell me about this place you visited, Obusah requested

"It's a day care center run by women."

"Its a woman's world, off course" Obusah remarked.

"I guess so. I tell you what, Talean was the head and all the staff were in their teens, real young women the whole staff was.

"Wo o, I wished I could visit a place like that. Next time you go, remember to take me along" Obusah said in a joyous voice. And without answering Eddie opened the door and let out Obusah first. He closed the door behind him and he went straight into the kitchen to make a cup of tea. He came into the dinning hall with the cup in his hands. He was greeted with cheers as a hero. He jacked his head back with surprise. "What was this? He asked himself. He did not know that Obusah had told every one in the dinning hall that he was out on a visit

"Wala!" one of the girls said. She looked down on her half empty plate. She took a spoonful, held it near her mouth. She turned round looked at Eddie again, and then pushed the spoon into her mouth slowly.

Eddie was a little embarrassed; he tried to make out what was happening. "Well, what was going on here? He asked.

"You were a great man" shouted one voice.

"You were the king of the jungle, "another voice said. The men were all jubilant. They all stopped eating.

The women looked on coldly and unmoved.

Eddie moved forward, sat down and took a sip of his tea. The lady next to him in her thirties, tuned round looked at Eddie. "What have you been doing today that this lot was praising you for?"

Eddie looked surprised. "Nothing actually" he replied. He looked straight into her eyes.

Kofi got up walked over to Eddie, bow before him." The king of the kingdom of strangers. I salute you sir."

"Nothing," the lady repeated. "They were not praising you for nothing. Confirm what you have been doing today."

"You got a lady friend in town today" the lady directly opposite Eddie said.

"No, not at all" he replied. "I went to visit a day care center that was all, nothing more than that. I am feeling my way in the big city.

"That alone deserved praise, doesn't it? The lady said. "We all just shuttle to and from the University campus each day. Boring though, but that was all we did. You have made contact, so you have some where to go for a change. None else do. That was a good start, keep it up" she said, then she got up and walked away.

Eddie got up walked towards the kitchen. Obusah was coming back from the kitchen into the dinning hall. He bowed before Eddie, saying I salute your greatness. This was repeated by another student behind Obusah.

"Stop being ridiculous" he told them. There was nothing unusual about going out of this place to see the city.

Any one else could do the same. It just happened that I did first." Eddie told them.

"Well, that puts the crown on your head" Obusah shouted with his mouth full of biscuits. A chorus of laughter followed. "None of us might never have that chance," another chorus of laughter.

Eddie shook his head, rolled his eyes and looked into the ceiling. He got up and walked out of the dinning hall without saying another word. He climbed the stair case and went into his room." I could not see the funny side of this event" he told himself. If I got anything going, it's nobody's business. Why should he in fact tell every body about what I am doing?" He was upset. He folded his mouth inwards. He kicked the chair he was going to sit on. "Bastard" the word came out forcefully. The chair fell, made a loud noise. Obusah who was coming up the stair had the noise, rushed into Eddie's room. "What happened?" he asked with a concerned voice. He looked at Eddie who now sat on the bed with his mouth still folded inwards. "You looked upset what went wrong?" he asked but Eddie said nothing. His face was still tense and flashes of anger showed on his eyes. "I have never seen you in this angry mode before. I knew that something was wrong. I heard a loud noise that was why I came in to find out. Eddie's face was still tense and his teeth still clenched, he told Obusah to F—off.

"Gee! Why were you swearing at me? I have not done nothing wrong, to come into your room after hearing loud noises. Have I? I thought you tripped and fell over, or some thing had gone wrong."

Eddie tried to control himself. "Why did you put my name on the line? If I went out of campus, it was none of your business to go and tell everybody about it in this flipping place. It was a private affair, why should every body in here knew about my personal affair? I have no business with any of these hobos and pussy clots, he said forcefully.

"Ah! was that why you were angry,? Go to hell man we are all in the same boat. We have to joke about each other and every one of us. Who really cared if you got angry? We needed to bring in news and joke about it. It happened that it was your turn today. Are you coming to the canteen by the way?" he asked Eddie.

"I might, but I am not too sure yet" Eddie replied. He got up and stood near the table.

"I would see you in the canteen" Obusah said and he rushed out of the room. Eddie still standing where he was and the chair still where it fell; he moved forward bent down and picked up the chair, pushed it under the table. He walked back to the bed, sat down again. He looked up to the ceiling, scratched his head as he tried to remember what to do next. He looked at himself, still in the dark shirt and sheep skin trousers and jacket. He remembered that he had not changed since he came back. "I should have changed my clothes ages ago, he got up again. "Oh gush, these shoes were killing me" he shouted. He kicked out his left shoe; while his trousers were still half way unbutton. He tried to unbutton his shirt in a hurry. "Let me do the shoes first he told himself. He loosen the shoes, took out the right shoe. The pain in the foot crept along his spine. "Oh gush" he shouted as he flung himself backwards on the bed. He held his foot high up in the air and he was soothing his foot when Obusah stormed back in a hurry, shouting. "Come on lets go to the canteen man." He entered the room in haste. He stopped suddenly when he saw Eddie on his back on the bed, half naked and his foot high up in the air. "Waite! What was going on here?" he asked in a surprised voice. "Why were you not dressed and sticking your foot in the air? " Obusah went on.

Eddie jumped from the bed, but could not get on his feet. He feel over as his trousers got between his knees and his shirt half way down his shoulders.

Obusah burst into loud laughter, which attracted Kim, who was on her way down the stairs to the kitchen.

She peeped and saw Eddie struggling to get up. "Were you lot playing kiddies games? She asked. F—off Eddie shouted. "I fell off my bed, and I am trying to get up.

"What were you doing that you were half undressed?' she asked. "You were in the hall moments ago, and now making a small show in your room. That was a bit naughty isn't it?" She walked away before Eddie got up.

His mouth was already folded into a nut ready to blow out dirty words, but Kim had gone. He came to the door; put his head out to see if she was still there. He came back into the room looked at Obusah with questioning eyes. "You scared me man; that was why I feel over" he told Obusah.

"Gee, me scare you? God forbid it. How did I scare you by the way? I came to call you to come to the canteen with me. I did not know a thing about what you were doing. Your door was half open, and so I just walked in" he said. "Get your self in order man and meet me at the canteen." He turned round and walked out.

Eddie was upset again. He kicked the chair again and punched the table. "Why should this woman see me half naked? She should not come into my room without knocking at the door? I hate her" he said in a furious voice. I would tell her off' he told himself, he jumped out of his trousers and let his shirt fell down his shoulders. He held the trousers and the shirt. He thought of the party trousers. "No man I did not need my sheep skin to go to the canteen. It could get soaked in cigarette smell. I am not changing these clothes now, no way" he said as he inspected them at arms length. "I am going out again" he said. He held the trousers at arms length, shook them, turned them round to have a good look, and then threw them on the bed.

He held the shirt, shook it and the looked at the collar. "It's not that dirty yet" he told himself, as he smelled it for sweat. He took the trousers folded them and put them on the pillow. He walked to the ward robe, took out a pair of jeans. He held them out for a few seconds, sat on the bed. He stretched his legs laid down and put his feet into the jeans slowly. He got up jumped to allow the jeans to come up to his waste. He buttoned up quickly. "I did not need to look into the mirror this time. I have no body to impress. He walked out of the room, still doing his buttons

"Ah! You were here at last, your highness" Obusah told Eddie jokingly. He walked to their table. The canteen was now full with students, all talking in groups. Eddie looked round the canteen, before he sat down. He could see that all the tables were occupied and a forest of beer glasses all half full.

His eyes caught the lady who walked into his room moments earlier in the evening. "I am going to tell her off in a minute. I did not care if she got upset. She upset me because I did not invite her. If she got nasty, I could throw my beer on her face. I did not care what happened. "He screwed his face as she turned round to look at him. He stopped by her smiled and then walked on. He stopped a few feet away, he tuned round again. "Hello, take your beer and come sit here by me, I have something to tell you" he said to her.

Obusah dragged Eddie to the table. "Sit there he told him.

Eddie sat reluctantly. He was still thinking about going to tell off the lady who just came into the canteen, and just talking with her friends.

By the way what was the name of that lady who came into my room this afternoon? There she walked into the canteen." He pointed at her with his mouth. "She was at the far end table with those women in bright African dresses. I am upset with you know. She came into my room without invitation. I wanted to F—her style off."

"She was Kim. She was a nice and friendly woman. She got on with everybody in the hostel, you know. You have not spoken to her yet? Obusah said.

Eddie shook his head "I am not interested in her anyway. She could go to hell. She was not beautiful" he added.

"Beautiful!" Obusah exclaimed. "We were not looking for beauty here my man. Any where I could, I would go get it.. You get what I mean? There was an old saying that "Dirty Water" could put out fire."

A chorus of laughter followed.

"So you did not look at the face?" asked John who had just joined the group.

"I support you Obusah" said Kofi. "If you are carrying a heavy bag full, you just want somewhere to empty it. A hungry man did not pick and choose. He ate anything offered to him." He added.

Eddie was not interested in the joke; he sat quietly, drinking his beer slowly.

"Are you for or against our argument?" John asked Eddie, looking straight into his eyes.

Eddie pulled his feet close and pushed them under his chair he replied "I have a taste for things, you know

If a woman was not attractive, I would not be tuned to her. I did not go for every dolly."

"Oh, no, "shouted John. "You have to be realistic, you were talking about an ideal situation, not the situation we were in now. It's more of a concentration camp here. He demonstrated with his hand. "Where we are" he continued "you could not afford to pick and choose. There were more men than women. None of us would like to go on and on without a friend." He said with emphasis.

Obusah rocked on his chair. "Yea man, you are right. You got desperate in this place," he said as he continued rocking on the chair. "We were all desperate folks, the idea of beauty would not come into your mind when you were that desperate. " Oh God help us" he put his hands on his face.

Eddie though desperate himself, but he would not share their concern. He remained calm and neutral, while the rest were a bit excited.

"I tell you what, if you were desperate and needed pressure release, you would not be sitting here you know Eddie told them in a calm voice

"Where would we go?" Obusah asked; his face close to Eddie's.

"He would eat you alive Eddie" shouted John. "If only you knew how desperate he was. "You tell us where to go.

"There was a place called Balsall Heath, you have lots of women waiting for men to pick them up. It's the red light district." Eddie told them.

"You sure about what you were saying Eddie even though we were black?" Obusah asked with a curious voice.

Eddie nodded his head, as he took a seep of his beer. "Yea man, you have lots of them all over the place. They lined up on the street outside their flats. Sometimes you see them on street corners and wave to you to come and talk to them. Some one told me about that place, you know. But I did not even know where the district actually was.

Honest. I did not know how to get there believe it or not. Alternatively, you could go into any pub and if you see a girl you fancied, you just go and sit by her and start a conversation."

"Suppose you talk about something she was not interested in? John asked.

"She would get up and walk away" Obusah replied laughing.

"But what about these women who were just sitting there by that table and nobody was talking to them." Kofi asked

"You could have a go at talking to them" Eddie told him.

"I am going over there to talk to them anyway" he said. He got up took his glass of beer and walked towards the table with four women sitting down and talking together.

He sat down on the empty chair between the women. The boys cheered him up, as he walked slowly and majestically towards the women. The lady sitting opposite the empty chair was in her thirties, she looked at the empty chair, then the approaching gentleman. The women looked at each other, and without saying a word. They each took their beer and drank it quickly. They got up one by one and left the table. They walked out of the pub.

Obusah threw his hands into the air, and then bang them on the table with loud noise. "What the F ... ing heck? He said in a disappointed voice. Every one turned round to look at John who drank his beer slowly, unconcerned with what was going on around him. He put the empty glass down, got up and walked slowly across the hall towards his friends. He drew out the chair next to Obusah and sat down.

"Well," Obusah said in a calm voice. "That was tough luck, wasn't it? Those stupid cows were not interested in you. You drove them out of the canteen.

"Never mind" said Eddie as he put his empty glass on the table. "You would have your luck some other time, may be not in this horrible place.

"But where would I go to get another luck? I would go no where" he said in an irritated voice. "I will not try it again, not these stupid she goats. No way; and not again, I hate them and I would not talk to any one of them again never. He raised his right hand and drew an imaginary line between him and them.

Eddie got up to go to the bar. "But John, that was not the end of the world, you have to keep trying, you have to carry on trying until you succeed." He walked to the bar to get another drink. He stood at the bar for a while. He walked towards the door.

"Keep on trying with insolent women, not me. I would not waste my flipping time on them again.

"Oh come on" Kofi said. "The women simply did not like your company that was why they got up and left. It would not matter to them, if you hated them, would it?"

"Oyea?" shouted Obusah. "You were leaving us, don't you?"

"Yes, I am going home to my room" Eddie replied and he walked to the door.

"But why don't you stay a little while, while we consoled this Prodigal son of Jobe. You should not snob him, you know." He got up walked quickly to the door, closed it before Eddie went out, he held Eddie's hand persuaded him to come back. He whispered into Eddie's right ear I have a joke for you and John, come back and listen to it. We should be leaving together." He looked at Eddie then smiled.

Edie stopped, made a quick look round the hall. "I am not walking away from you, you know. I just felt tired and wanted to go to my bed. You get what I mean?' he said softly.

"Oh gush, it's too early to go to bed, man. You should not run away from the fun at this early hour." Obusah told him.

"Too early," Eddie repeated. "You must be joking. It's nearly eleven o'clock The canteen should be closing in half an hours time," he replied in a loud voice,

"Yes, you were right, but stick with us for more round of drinks. I get you a pint right away." They walked back, as Obusah pulled his hand. Obusah walked quickly passed him to the bar. Eddie looked round once more before he sat down. His eyes caught up with a lady in the next table by the window. She smiled at Eddie. He cracked his brain trying to remember where he had met her. Obusah pushed the beer glass towards him. Eddie got up and walked towards the table.

"Where are you going? Here is your beer" Obusah said in a raised voice.

"Just a minute" he replied. He replied as he walked towards the lady who had now glued her eyes on him.

The three men on the tables who were all white exchanged glances and one of them in his twenties screwed his eyes in disgust, turned to the lady. "Is he coming to talk to you?" she nodded. "I knew him before".

"You knew him? He asked in a disappointing voice, and screwed his nose with contempt.

Edie came close, bent over the lady to talk to her.

The guy got up took his wine glass, moved to the other table in silent protest.

"Hi, we have met before haven't we?" Eddie said to her.

"Yes" she replied with a broad smile. "We met at the Trees, and you bought me a drink. You alright?" she asked.

"Yes, man I am fine." He replied

"Sit down" she said to Eddie.

He sat down for a short while. The two white folks made glances at each other, giving negative vibes to Eddie.

"Why not come and sit with us on that table?" Eddie asked her with a smile. Eddie's friends have been watching him from a distance. "Alright" she replied. "I am coming over with you. Eddie got up and walked back to their table. The lady got up to follow Eddie. One of the guys put his hand over her to stop her moving "do not follow that black bastard. But with a stern look on her face she said "let go my hand now" in a furious voice. She clenched her fist and her teeth. She got up saying nothing to the two gentlemen.. One of them shouted "bastard" as she walked away.

The lady turn round abruptly, and without saying a word, but her posture, the position of her mouth and eyes spoke clearly. She turned round again and went to sit down with Eddie and friends.

"Welcome, Obusah said to her. "Well done "Eddie you have saved the day for us. You see guys Eddie was a real fisherman, he knew where to catch the big fishes." He said jokingly.

"You alright?" Eddie asked her as he looked into her face wearing sad and disgusting looks.

She shuffled her self. "You see those guys they were a racist lot and they were trying to stop me from moving from their table, and one of them shouted behind me bastard. I was walking away from them when the shout came and I did not know who said the word. They called me names. But I don't care. I like black people. I get on well with them. I had a black boy friend before. He took good care of me. I hated that lot ooh. They were just wind bags." She took a sip of her beer.

"Never mind" Eddie said to her as he nudged her shoulder and pulled her slightly towards him.

"You were in safe hands. We cared and respect women.

"I get you a drink" Eddie told her, as he got up and walked towards the bar.

"Oh please" she said with a smile. "Brandy and ice" she shouted behind him. "You alright boys?" she asked, looking at the two men sitting directly opposite her.

They both looked stunned and speechless. They were both stirring at her. "Why don't you say something? My name is Olivia. What is your name?" turning to the man on her left.

"John" he replied.

"Do you know that lots of people have funny ideas about Africa and Africans. But I didn't mind being in the company of Africans. They were loving and caring people. You liked it here with all these flipping racist lot around you." She asked.

Obusah shrucked his shoulders, open his arms without saying a word.

Eddie showed an indifferent attitude.

"I am here for one thing only" said John. "I didn't intend living here. I do not go to nobody's house. Racist or not, the sooner I got what I came here for the better and I would be on my way home to my family and job."

He took his glass and took a deep drink from it and put it down again.

Olivia turned to Eddie looked at him for a while "What have you been doing to your self since I last saw you in the Trees? You have put on lots of weight." She said weighing Eddie's left arm and checking his Tommy.

Eddie was still digging his mind to get her name. But he could not put a finger on the details of the meeting. She had told the other fellows her name.

"Olivia," Obusah called out "where were your friends?"

"I have no friends, honest, those girls we hang out were girls we meet only occasionally. We did not hang out together all the time.

Eddie quickly remembered her face and how they met at the Trees pub on Bristol road in High Gate.

"Nothing special" he replied smiling, just having a bit of good time and studying. I should be losing weight really, because I spent long hours in the library and stayed up late most times reading." He took a seep of his beer, wipe his mouth. He looked straight at Obusah who had his eyes glued at Olivia in admiration.

"I admire you Africans, you know. You are very clever. All Africans came here to study for sure. They were all educated people and hard working lot, unlike the West Indians who spend most of their time lolling about. Why were you so clever? What did you eat in Africa that made you clever? I wanted to go to Africa so that I too would become clever like you lot.

Obusah pulled his feet together. He changed his position, and supported his head with both hands, with the elbows on the table. "Nothing really, we all have different foods that we ate, depending on the country you came from". We all just eat our African food stuffs and nothing else. But we have to work very hard to earn our living. There is no social security in Africa."

Olivia who was fiddling with Eddie's fingers looked straight at Obusah with astonishment. "You were joking" she told him. "If there was no social security in Africa, how did people like us survive? What did the government do for them people who have no education and did not go to work? Didn't the government give money to people who could not support themselves?"

Eddie shook his head. No body received any money from the government without working hard for it The word unemployment did not exist in Africa and that was the bitter truth. If you did not work, you have to depend on your relatives for everything. If anybody told you that there was social security in Africa he was telling you a lie

Olivia looked bewildered. She crossed her legs, supported her head with her left hand and looked into Eddie's eyes. "What did your government do for old and sick people and the like. They let them die on the street? I would never go to a place like that, no way." She smiled and said "Well, not really. If I got married to an African, I would come visit his home. I would have to cook him dinner, clean up the house and looked after his old relatives. Your wife look after all your relatives in Africa, is that true? "She looked at Obusah again.

"Yes, that was true" replied John. "My wife looked after my mother and father. Sometimes relatives came for a visit. She had to cook for them. So if you got married to an African like Eddie, you have to learn to look after his relatives.

Olivia looked at Eddie's face smiling. "But you lot were all married to African women weren't you?" she asked. She looked at each man's face.

"I have a wife with two children" said John.

"I have a wife with three children, tow girls and one boy" said Obusah.

She looked at Eddie in the eye. "I have no wife and no kids. Eddie said. She looked into Eddie eye to eye with questioning eyes. "You sure you were not married. Every African that came here would say he was not married, even though they had a wife waiting for them" she said in a disgusting voice.

"That was not true for every African" Eddie replied in an irritated voice.

"Yes that was true" she said, looking at him with stern eyes" I have been told by many people that, that was the case. They came here got married to a white woman, have children, then went back to their African wives."

Eddie' face changed, showing signs of anger. Olivia relaxed into her seat. She put her hand on her chest. "Have I upset you? Don't be upset. I am just saying the truth. I knew many white women who have had children who had gone back, and were living with their African women. Some women have gone to African to prove their point." she said in an agitated voice.

"I have been living here for three years now. If I had a wife and children, they should have been here with me. It was unfair to leave you family for so long" Eddie said.

"But suppose you did not want them to join you here? You see what I mean? She added.

"Oye, let us leave this subject and drink our beer" said Obusah. "If you liked Eddie, you would not listen to what people who know nothing about Africa tell you. They said that if you listened to the noises in the market you would never buy anything

"We saw pictures of Africa all the time on the Television.

"Oh no, please, do not talk about the pictures you see over here about Africa, They gave you what they want you to see, not the real picture of what Africa is today. There were pockets of poverty here and there. That was true just like here." John told her.

"You were true, you know. My best friend went to Africa on holiday, and she said she liked the place. She had gone to live there. She had even got married with two children. She came last year to see her parents. She said she would never come to live here again. I wanted to visit Africa, but I have no money and no one to take me there" she said in a begging voice with clenched fists.

"You have got the right man by your side to take you there" John said jokingly.

With a big smile, she looked at Eddie, patted his cheek, and then turned to Obusah. "He did not love me, honest.

"He does" said John. "Yes, he loved you. He would take you to Sierra Leone."

"Sierra Leone" she repeated. "I would if he was taking me." She turned abruptly to Eddie with pleading eyes. You like me? Would you take me to your country? I liked you, you know. She raised her head and kissed his left cheek.

Obusah and John cheered Eddie up. "This woman is all for you Eddie" John said in a manly voice. You should take her with you when you go on holidays.

Obusah got up and shook Eddie's hand. He took Olivia's right hand and placed it in Eddie's left palm, folded both, saying "I bless you too and your friendship." He went back to his seat, took his beer glass, told John to take his and said we drink to the health of you two.

Olivia rested her elbows on Eddie's thighs, said "Thank you Obusah. I love to marry to an African, you know. She squeezed her head on Eddie's shoulder. She looked up at Eddie. Guess what, those white bastards hate that you know. They do not want us to talk to you lot West Indian men are jealous of you lot too. They hated you and said all nasty things about you." She got up saying "excuse me; I am going to the toilet."

As she disappeared into the toilet, Obusah exclaimed "Oh God bless me. This woman was in love with you Eddie. Take good care of her."

"Well, I understand this lot. They fall in love very easily. They equally come out of it as easily as came into it. They get upset quite easily. The bad thing about them was that any little thing will turn her off." Eddie said in a calm and quiet voice.

"Well, you should not upset her then, once you know who you were dealing with." John told him.

Eddie shook his head slowly "no deal in the works. She would tell you any way.

"Olivia was a nice girl you know Obusah told Eddie.

Eddie nodded his head as he seeped his last bit of beer.

Olivia came back in a hurry. "I heard the bell while I was in the toilet. I just finish my drink, and then you come with me to the bus stop. Will you?" She looked at Eddie

"We will take you to the bus stop and put you on the bus before we go to our rooms" said Obusah.

"Oh thank you, you were real gentlemen. She held on to Eddie's hand as they got up she needed a bit of support. She put most of her weight on Eddie's shoulder. He turned round looked at her. "You are drunk aren't you? "he asked looking at Olivia whose eyes were flushed and sleepy looking.

"Well, not really, I am just a bit tipsy" she replied in a slurred voice. "I have been drinking with that lot before I saw you and you have given me too much brandy and I did not want to waste it. I am alright though, I can get home alright. No man is going to full around with me you know. I will call the police, trust me. I am going to get down the bus walk down the street and take the lift to the fifth floor. I have my house key here. "She took it out and showed it to Eddie. She fiddled with them, and then said this is my front door key.

"You better take this woman home. She has had more than enough drink tonight. That was more than her head could hold. I bet she will miss her bus stop," Obusah said to Eddie. She was missing her steps now and again and her voice was fading and words coming out in spots and disjointed.

"No, no way, I am going home alone. I don't want any man to follow me into my flat. I am not stupid. I know what I am doing. Eddie can come over and visit me tomorrow, day time or when ever. I lived on the fifth floor at Inkerman house, flat number fifty one. You could come tomorrow day time right, when I am sober. We can have a drink and talk. I will make you a lovely cup of tea. I know how to make good tea trust me. I went on a course and they taught us how to make tea. You are coming to visit me tomorrow right? She hugged Eddie, putting all her weight on him.

"Yes, I would come over" he replied. "Are you on the phone so that I call first to make sure that you were there before I turned up?"

"No, I am not on the phone. I could not afford a phone in my flat. I would stay home and wait for you. Hurry up the bus was coming" she told Eddie. As she tried to run, she fell.

"Bops" Obusah shouted, as Olivia fell on the pavement like a bag.

Eddie helped her up, brushed her jeans and blouse. "You alright?" he asked.

"Yes, I am fine, thanks," she replied

"Can you get home alright? "He asked her as he helped her into the bus.

"I would get home alright. Thank you boys; I see you tomorrow. She went into the bus, waved to them, and staggered to the seat.

The bus pulled away.

"I bet she was going to sleep on the bus. The men walked back to the hostel,

"Well. If she did we could not do nothing about it, could we?" Eddie exclaimed.

They walked in silence for a while, "It's not a bad evening was it?" asked John

"It's Eddie's night man John" Obusah replied jokingly.

"Don't start please, let us go home and get into our beds.

CHAPTER 20

▼

The men walked in silence for a while. They got to the front door. Eddie opened the door. John rushed in

"I am going straight to my bed." He said.

"You were going to your bed at this time of night? Obusah asked in a raised voice. "I am going to the kitchen. I feel a bit peckish. Are you coming John?" he asked.

"No, no food down my throat again at this hour." John replied as he heads for the stairs.

Eddie rushed up stairs, opened his door, and closed it in a hurry without looking.. He turned the light on.

After a brief look around, he sat on the bed, he was trying to remember the evening's events. He was at the same time undoing the buttons of his shirt.

There was a knock at the door. Who could it be? He thought. He got up to go and open the door. "I wished Obusah could leave me alone now. I hoped he was not bringing a plate full of rice into my room at this hour of the night.

He opened the door and held it. It was Ms Osborne. "A phone call for you" she said and walked away.

"Oh thank you" he said as he ran down the stairs to the hall. As he took the receiver, he could hear Obusah's voice in the distance.

"Hello, where have you been. This was the fourth time I am calling. You go gallivanting all over the place.. You were never in your room. What have you been doing?" Talean's voice on the other end.

"I went to the canteen with my friends. We just came back actually," Eddie replied.

"You drunk now weren't you?" she asked jokingly.

"No man, not really; I did not drink to get drunk. I hated the hang over the next day, so I just drink enough to feel fine" he told her.

"Oh, you feeling fine now, aren't you? I had a rough day today, I am feeling really tired. But I wanted to talk to you before I went to my bed. I was getting worried about you, you know. I thought something might happen to you, you get what I mean? You take good care of your self, will you? Do not go all over the place drinking. It's not good for your health. If I was there I would control your drinking. Who and who went out with you to the bar? "She asked. Eddie shrucked his shoulders and twisted his mouth

"Just the three of us" he replied.

"You really sure about that? She asked laughing

Eddie got a bit edgy "What were you trying to say. I did not know many people in this hostel. You know"

"But you know at least one lady in there. I bet you. do."

"No not at all" he replied in an angry voice. "I do not have the time to go round looking for friends. I have better things to think about." He added.

"Yes, your studies and me isn't it?" she joked. "You cannot divide your attention between me and another woman. If you do and I find out I will kill you. How did you spend you day anyway? She asked ina soft and condescending voice.

Eddie looked at his watch, then the clock on the wall. "Well, nothing special I went to the library came home cook my dinner. I ate then watch television. We played cards. I had one hour rest, and then we went to the canteen

"That was a good normal day. What did you have for dinner?' she asked. I had pork stew and mixed vegetables and brown rice.

"Hmmm, that sounds nice" she said in a quick tone. You like pork. I know that very well.

Guess what, I might be late for the morning lecture tomorrow. I have to meet a parent in the center tomorrow morning. She might not turn up on time as it is usual with black people. They normally turn up for an appointment one hour late, with excuses,

.Listen Talean, you did not have to attend every lecture, you know. especially when you know that you were not up to it. You get what I mean? You were expected to attend up to eighty percent. You would not miss anything, trust me. I would be there on time and I would feed you up with the details later on" he told her in a confident and calm voice.

She giggled and made some audible voices on the phone. "You were a God send friend. You know. I could not do without you in this course, with a head two planks thick,. I just could not manage it on my own, you understand what I mean' It's all easy for you. You may not believe it, I was reading that book the other day, it was all Greek to me, honest. I could not even understand what they were trying to explain. I just switched off completely. I then closed the book and turned the light off and went to sleep. You have the brains to read and understand what ever you were reading, I did not, honest. Listen, I wanted to come by you after lectures tomorrow. Can I?" she asked in a low voice

Eddie shifted his weight from one leg to the other. His face brightened with smiles "Yea man; that will be fine. I have nothing planned, any way." he told her.

"You sure you wanted to see me at your place? She asked. "I would stay as long as you wanted, and I would help you cook your dinner. Would you like me to cook for you, or you cook your dinner or both of us do the cooking together?" She asked

Eddie changed his position one more time. The door opened, Obusah pushed his head in. "Are you still on the phone? Spotty little cat leave the phone for other people to use. You have been greedy with the phone you know.

"We would cook together and eat together." he told her.

"Oh hooo, that sounded nice. I look forward to that. Who was speaking in the back ground? She asked.

"It's Obusah, that stupid little prick. Eddie told her.

"Is he your friend?" she asked.

"Yes' he replied as he waved Obusah good night.

"What was he saying, I heard him mention the phone. Have I been talking too long? Did he want to use the phone? She asked

"No, he did not want to use it, he was just been a thorn in my ass. He was just looking for something to say. He was gone to his bed already.

"I thought I am hanging on the phone, while other students wanted to use it." she said in a cautious voice.

No, not at this time of night, most people had gone to bed. He had just been to the kitchen to eat." He told her.

Eating at this time of night? It's a bit too late wasn't it? Well, I do get peckish late at night sometime and I had to eat.

If I eat food at this time of night, I would be a Billy frog tomorrow.

"What were you saying? You mean you could not eat solid food in the night? Won't you eat if you went to a party?

"I have a poor digestive system. Food took a lot longer in my Tommy. If I did not eat early, it would not be digested at all." He changed his position one more time.

The door opened, Mrs. Osborne the matron came out to close the front door. "Remember to turn off this light, before you go to bed." She told him quietly.

"Yes, I will he replied.

"Who was that? She asked.

"The matron she was telling me to turn off the light before I go up to my room.

"I must go then. It seemed every one had gone to bed. I felt bored sometimes sitting here alone doing nothing, and nobody to talk to"

What about Mr. and Mrs. Howard.

Oh gush, do not talk about those people. They were in bed as soon as it got dark. Me and them hardly have time together. They would be sleeping while we were talking. I see you in the morning. Sleep well. I give you a good night kiss on the phone.

Yes, I will have it tonight and tomorrow." he said giggling

Good night" she said and dropped the phone.

As Eddie dropped the receiver, he saw Mrs. Osborne walked passed towards the dinning hall. "That was a long conversation wasn't it? She said to Eddie.

Without saying a word, he walked quickly up to his room, doubling the stairs. He kicked the door open, threw himself into his bed. He kicked the shoes off his feet, and then pushed himself under his bed linens. "A dinner together with Mrs. Hill, and then an evening together would be great. He closed his eyes and dosed off.

It was early in the morning when Obusah came to Eddie's room. Eddie was still in bed with half open eyes. He was just whiling away his time in bed and his eyes were still heavy. "You were still in bed?" Obusah said to him.

"Yea man I am just resting. I am not really sleeping but I felt a little bit tired, that is all.

"You have an appointment today, do you remember? Obusah told him.

"Yea man I still remember, but do not put all your eggs in a single basket. She might have forgotten about us, by the time she got home. I remember." he replied in an unsure voice.

"Yes you might be right. We did not tell her where we lived as a matter of fact. He hit his forehead with his palm. I now remember, I did tell her that" he said in a cool voice. "But remember also that she knew that we are students, and lived in a hostel. I do remember she asked us about where we lived, and I surely told her.

So if she did not see you she might come look for you. Mrs. Osborne will show her your room, trust me. You better honor the invitation.

It was still quite early morning, but the noise from the corridor by the toilet got louder and louder. It forced Eddie to get up. He tried to force himself to lay still, while trying to make out the voices seeping into his room. He raised his head slightly up, strained his ears, and then put his head back on the pillow. He tried to remember what he did last night.

Eddie then got up, sat on the side of the bed. He looked round, and still confused about what to do.

"You are going, aren't you? Obusah asked. He now held the door to go out.

Eddie got up stretched himself, with a big yawn. "Anyway, I would try and make it to her place. The fact was that if a woman invited you to her place, she really meant business. Otherwise, she will not tell you where she lived."

Obusah went out and rushed down stairs.

CHAPTER 21

▼

It was early next morning, Eddie got up stretched himself and then looked out through the window. "Oh gush it was still Wednesday today" he mourned

He was still sleepy, but the early morning rush hour had already begun. The queue outside the toilet was getting longer and longer. Some students took unusually long time in the toilet. They kept the rest of the students waiting outside. There had been moments when a student badly needed to go and have a wee and furiously banging the toilet door. There had even been occasions when there was swearing outside the door. Eddie had tried to avoid this by using the toilet very early before any one got up and went back to his bed, and Obusah had called him early bird.

Eddie could not go back to sleep, because of the noise outside his door. The toilet was just opposite his door.

He rubbed his eyes and looked at the clock which was just striking eight o'clock. "Oh gush, I am late getting up. He jumped out of his pajamas and into his flip flop.

The noise outside had died down, he emerged from his room went into the toilet. He emerged from the loo and walked back quickly into his room. He hurriedly changed into his brown sheep shin trousers, a striped shirt and brown and gold colored tie. As he looked into the morrow, he thought the tie did not go well with the shirt and the trousers. "Qui bon" he said to himself. "Nobody was going to care, but may be Talean would care. I am not changing anything anyway he told himself. I am getting late." He rushed downstairs into the kitchen to prepare breakfast. He was doing every thing in a hurry, spilling sugar and corn flakes.

"You alright?" one lady asked. Eddie looked round, she smiled. He nodded, and then looked at her friend standing next to her. They looked at each other and laughed.

Eddie ignored them, carried on stirring his tea. Suddenly he felt a tap on his right shoulder. He turned round, Obusah smiled. "You looked smart, but not quite. Did you have a look at your mirror this morning?

"Of course I do every morning." he replied in an upset voice.

"But you did not this morning. Did you?"

"I did man. What were you trying to tell me?" he said angrily.

"Have you gone Rastafara? Obusah taunted

Eddie realized that he did not comb his head. It was a bad start of the day he though. No wonder those pussy clots were goggling. They thought I had gone barmy this morning.

The two ladies burst out laughing.

Eddie stamped his right foot. "I combed my hair man before I left my room.

"You did very badly and perhaps too hurriedly" one of the ladies said laughing..

"You tell him" Obusah said to her.

"You forgot to comb your head. It's like a child just getting up from sleep in the morning That was alright for a Rasta, I suppose I am sure you were not one of them, am I right?" she said in a soft voice with smiles.

Eddie's face tightened with anger, the tea cup in his hands slipped and crashed on the floor.

"Oh ho, "Obusah exclaimed, as he moved away from the flying glass and tea sprays. "We have not caused that have we? The lady said as she moved closer, knelt down to pick the pieces of enamel, while the other lady rushed for the mop.

She got up, and offered him her cup of tea. "Shall I make you another cuppa? Eddie nodded.

"I would do you breakfast as well, if you tell me what you wanted to have" she offered.

"That was very kind of you" Eddie told her.

"Yes my dear, you needed a helping hand this morning" Obusah added, as he took his breakfast plate into the dinning room.

"Why don't you go and comb your hair, while she prepared you another breakfast plate?"

"That was an idea" he thought. And without saying another word he left the kitchen and walked quickly into his room to comb his hair. Eddie was still convinced that his head was in fact combed.

He looked into the mirror. "Oh gush," he exclaimed, as he saw his hair in a mosaic of tiny curls. If I had gone out like that, people would think that I have gone barmy. How come I did not remember to comb my hair? He was looking through his timetable when a ladies voice spiraled up the stairs into his room. "Eddie, your break fast was ready. Come and get it" he took his bag and rushed down stairs, through the dinning hall into the kitchen. He came back into the dinning hall; put his bag on the empty chair by John. He was walking towards the kitchen when he heard some one say. "Louise was waiting for you in the Kitchen. Hurry up little spoiled brat. Eddie stopped and turned round to see who was speaking. A smile from Louise's friend Audrey who was drinking her tea on the table in the left corner on the entrance to the hall..

Louise was holding the dinner plate in her hands as Eddie walked towards Her.

She smile, then said "there you are stretching her arms. I hope that would do for the morning

With a broad smile, Eddie stretched his hands to receive the plate. "This was a big breakfast, thanks a lot."

He said to her. He turned round and walked to the dinning hall. He transferred the plate to his left hand. He put the plate on the table, put the bag on the floor, then drew a chair and sat down. He took the fork and knife, surveyed the contents of the plate pouched eggs, fried bacon, baked beans four toasts and a lump of butter. This was what one would need every morning, a woman to do your breakfast. But who cares for any one in this place. They would not even allow us to bring women friends into our room, or beer. It's a shame that they treated adults like us as if we were in a youth camp. I did what I liked anyway. There was always beer in my room.

While Eddie was eating, Louise walked passed. She stopped by Eddie "Was it alright?" She asked.

"It's the best breakfast, I have had for ages" he answered as he held the toast with both hands and biting it in mouth fulls.

"That was good, have a nice day" she said.

"I wished I could have this every morning" he told Louise with out looking at her. But she was gone, when he turned round to look at her. "Oh she was gone already." He took his last bite, and then mourned "This was a bit too much. I did not have to eat all of it" he told himself.

He got up took the plate into the kitchen, pour the left overs into the bin, washed the plate. As he wiped his hands on the hand towel, he looked at his watch. "It's already 8.55. I have only five minutes to get into the University, in time for the lecture. He rushed back into the hall, took his bag and made for the front door. . "It did not really matter if I go late into the lecture. Oh gush, I am leaving Talean's folder. She would kill me if I left it behind." He ran back upstairs to get it; he opened the door in a hurry, rushed into the room, looked round for the folder. He started shifting the books on the table round. By the time he found the folder, the table was in a mess. He took the folder, held it and stepped back to look at the table. "It was a disgrace, if anyone came in here and saw the table like that. But I have no time now to pack it. I would do that when I came back

He rushed out of the room, bang the door and ran down the stairs towards the front door and he remembered that his bag was on the bed. "Oh gush, I am going barmy this morning." he told himself. He unlocked the door after swearing aloud. He turned round and saw Mrs. Osborne standing by with a surprised face. The lady cleaner looked at Eddie with a frown. He looked at them; the lady cleaner in her forties had her mouth folded inwards firmly. She blinked her eyes, while Mrs. Osborne stood motionless.

"You alright?" Mrs. Osborne asked. "Sort of" Eddie replied. Without another exchange of words, they walked passed.

Eddie went into his room, took his bag, put the folder inside it, zip it, then put his head out of the door to see if Mrs. Osborne was still around. He came out lock the door. "They should go about their flipping business, these pussy clots. " He walked down the stairs slowly, and out into the street.

As he turn round the corner into Weston Road, he heard the big clock at the University striking nine o'clock.. "I wish Dr, Ryan would be late again today. He came late all the time anyway. So I would not miss anything.

Eddie was crossing the Bristol road when a bus pulled up from the city. He ran across to the other side of the busy road. He walked passed the bank, when he heard a soft voice calling him from behind. That was Talean he told himself. He moved to the edge to allow the flood of students to pass by. He then turned round in time to provide a pillar for Talean who needed support after running across the busy road, trying to catch up with him. She was out of breath, as she put all her weight on his left shoulder and resting her head. After regaining her breath, she told him "I had to run with the rest of the students across the road. I am not used to running, you know." She was still breathing heavily. Every part of my body was breathing" she told him.

"You needed exercises sometimes, you know. That would be good for your health.

"Eh, eh, not when I did not have free time to myself. If I was not here, I would be at the center or at home doing some work. But you were late Eddie" she told him as she looked into his eyes. She pushed his hand urging him to move on. "Come on let us be going. We were already late for the lecture. He turned round to her, "I was waiting for you to regain your breath. You were alright now, I suppose." He moved on with her hand still in his. She nodded as they walked slowly amid crowds of students streaming to the campus. She let go his hand as he was digging her palm with his thumb. After releasing her hand from his firm grip, she stretched her fingers, and then pushed her hand into her side pocket.

"I could not leave on time, because I got up late, and by the time I had breakfast, it already past eight thirty. You know we have to queue up for the toilet and the cookers in the kitchen each morning. It's a disgrace wasn't it? I mean you pay for those facilities. Why do you have to queue for the toilet. Was it because all the people in the hostel were black people and they all came from third world countries and so they could treat you any way and you would not complain."

"I tell you what, I would complain to the University authorities" she told him

"But what would they do? It's a private hostel, not controlled by the University. They were actually doing the University a favor, by accepting students." He said as they walked past the crowds to the road leading to the Education Building.

"But the hostel depended on the University for their very existence. If there were no students to accommodate those lots will go down to the dole." she added.

They walked on more slowly now with less people on the foot road. "I was expecting you much later" he told her. "How come you came so early?" Eddie asked, pulling Talean close with his left hand.

There was brief silence. He looked at her. Mrs. McCallum did not turn up for the meeting. She rang up to say that her daughter was having runs. So I decided to come and surprise you. Are you not happy to see me now?" She looked into his eyes with a big smile.

Eddie stopped looked into her eyes. The chemistry was at work as they gazed at each other. Eddie's mind was wondering, as he looked closely at Talean. She pulled her eyes in a romantic fashion. She must be looking out for a kiss he thought. They both remain silent but the looks on each face spoke in clear language. The flame of passion was burning brightly in each face. Eddie looked round to see if any one was looking. She moved on by the time he turned round to her.

"Move on" she told him. Without saying a word, Eddie realized that he was in the middle of the road, students and lectures were moving in all directions. He put his head down, and walked on slowly. Talean had moved a few feet away from him. She urged him to hurry up. "We were late for the lecture, you know." She told him.

"Oh dam it. It did not matter when we got there. He came late for the lecture nearly all the time, and he was the worst lecturer anyway among the lot. His lecture always bored me to sleep. I would rather sit in the library and read about the topic than listen to his lecture."

They walked on. "You were right you know. I never got nothing from his lectures. I understand better when I read the text book or journal. But I get more confused at the end of the lecture. But we have to be present in the lecture even if we got nothing out of it except confusion.

Eddie and Talean walked through the two double glass doors. They saw Dr Hughes coming in. "That was him" Talean whispered into Eddie's ear. They looked at each other and smiled without saying a word.

"You see what I mean. He never came on time." Eddie told her in a quiet voice.

The lift doors opened. Eddie moved forward to get into the lift. Talean pulled back his jacket. He turned round to look at her. "Do not go on the lift with him" she whispered into his ear. "Let's wait for the next lift or use the stairs."

"Stairs! F..ing hell. Climb those stairs to the fifth floor? No way" he told her.

"Come on in "Dr Hughes told Eddie and Talean. She was standing behind Eddie, partially holding her face behind his jacket. They both looked at the lecturer and smiled. "We were waiting for a friend" she told Dr. Hughes in a soft voice with smiles.

You were not coming in for my lecture then.

"Yes we are" they both said together.

"I see you in a bit then" he let go the lift holding button and the doors closed.

The lift came back. There were too many people waiting for the lift. You would miss it if you did not rush for it. Eddie moved in first, followed closely behind by Talean and many other students. They stood in silence for a while. It's a bit choky in here" he said "There was plenty of room in that lift ride you know. You would miss this again if you did not rush to get in since there were many people waiting to use the lift" he told her.

"Yes, I do know that, but I did not want to ride the lift with Dr. Hughes. He was our lecturer. You should avoid close contact with these people. I hated to stand face to face with them. "She was fanning her nose all the time as she spoke. "You get what I mean." she told him.

"What were you saying?" Eddie pulled her close. "You mean he.… Eddie twisted his nose and screwed his facial muscles.

"Yes, last time I had a closed encounter with him, he had the smell of alcohol and a skunky breath. I did not want to go through that again this morning he said in a very low voice. She moved close to Eddie, and whispered into his ear again. "Stop it, will you? People were listening." She put her index finger over her mouth as he opened his mouth to speak again. The lift doors opened. Eddie moved out first and the rest of the people walked out. They walked to the lecture room, Talean following Eddie closely. He walked straight into room 501followed by Talean. Quietly and without attracting any attention, they tiptoed to the nearest back seat close to the door. They sat down.

The lecturer was still doing the attendance.

"You see what I mean? He was still not ready yet. Eddie whispered to Talean.

What a hopeless man she said to herself.

Eddie was trying to mumble something to her; she put her finger over her mouth to tell him to shut up.

Eddie sat quietly while Dr Hughes explained the introduction to the topic and the work sheet he handed out.

Talean glanced through the hand out. She tried to read it and listen to the explanations, but she decided to listen to the explanation. I would read this later on after the lecture. She looked round the room. Everyone seemed to be listening. Two students closed by were talking Tet a tet quietly.

Eddie sat leaning on the chair with his hands folded across his chest and his legs were stretched at full length. He looked straight at the lecturer. The room was half full, all listening and some taking notes As the students got up to collect the reading list, Eddie too got up. He told Talean to sit back while he went to collect the handouts.

"Thank God it's all over" Talean said, as she walked out of the lecture room first, followed by Eddie. "It's the most boring Lecture each week" she told Eddie. "I know" He replied. He waffles a lot. He never prepared for any of these lectures. I wonder why he got paid at all for doing nothing."

"He is a Doctor, you know." She told Eddie.

"And so what a man's title did not tell you was whether the man knew what he was doing. You have people like him in every institution. I only attend his lecture because I have to, and I could not change subjects now. I have been told that we just have to stick with it, regardless of what we think about the course.

"But he gave us handouts and reading lists" she said, as they walked towards the lift. "We are going to the library, aren't we?"

Eddie nodded, as they entered the lift. "We are not staying long though, we just get some books to read on this topic, then we go to mine." he told her.

They walked out of the lift and turn round to go into the library. "I knew that I am going to help you cook your dinner today.

Eddie hit his head with his right hand. "Oh yea, I remembered now. You promised to cook for me today."

She stopped looked at him. "Oh Eddie, have you forgotten already. I have been looking forward to it, you know. You were not interested were you?" She pulled his hand to stop him, as they walked to the library door

He stopped turned round and smiled. "I was just pulling your leg." He said to her.

You were not, you have really forgotten. You were not that interested, honest" she said in an upset voice, her mouth in a tiny round shape. She lifted her head up, looked at him with doubtful eyes, and without saying a word, but she was seeking a definite decision from him.

He put his hand on her shoulder in a gentle and reassuring manner. He smiled with broad happy face and then said "I did not want to show how anxious I am about us being together this afternoon.

"You sure you wanted me to come spend the afternoon with you?" She still had doubts in her face.

"Stop being a doubting Thomas, you know I love you and look forward to being with you.

She looked around, put her finger over her mouth. Her face changed to a regret full look. "I should not have given out my secret away, she thought. She looked at him again for signs of disapproval. She was still upset with herself. She blamed herself for telling him her mind. She breath deep and fast.

Eddie moved on through the door and across the barrier. He looked back and she was still standing outside the door. He called out and beckoned to her to follow.

Eddie saw John walking towards the library. She smiled as John touched her left shoulder. "I was just watching him go through the barrier" she told John.

"You finished for the day?" he asked. "Yea man we have the only lecture for the day.

"Luck you; I have two more to go. I would see you later. I am rushing to my next lecture. I just came by when I saw you standing still and alone." He noticed the change of mode in both her face and posture and decided not in intervene.

"Tra" Eddie shouted while Talean waved with a false smile.

Eddie came out to meet John, and took Taleans left hand "come on lets go into the library, He pulled her hand. "Oh, before I forget. I bought some Brandy the other day for me and you." He said in a loud voice without realizing where they were. They went through the barrier into the library.

What were you looking forward to? She asked, as she doubled her steps to keep up with his long strides. "Don't drag me along, walk slowly man, you are not going to catch a runaway train. Are you? Tell me" she urged him.

CHAPTER 22

▼

Eddie and Talean walked into the library in silence for a while. They walked pass the issue desk and straight to the reference section. 'What were you looking forward to today?" she asked again as she stood behind him in the catalogue boxes. Eddie was busy looking through the reference catalogue. "Don't you have anything to say?" she shook his shoulder.

"Oh, before I forget, I bought a Brandy bottle for you and I the other day,

"Hush" she put her index finger over his mouth to tell him to shut up. Why were you repeating this Brandy bottle talk inside the library after you already talked about it outside the library minutes ago? She asked him in a very low voice.

Eddie closed the catalogue draw and they walked up to the first floor. "You sit down" he told her pointing to the empty table. She put her folder down, drew out the chair and sat down. She fiddled with the folder, just pretending to do something. Eddie had disappeared behind the book stacks. Talean shuffled her folder, looking for a document. She sat quietly, reading through one computer print out on the A4 sheet.

Eddie ran his eyes through the books on the shelves like a scanner. He took one, looked at its contents, put it back. He continued scanning. "Oh yes, this book was gone. Someone had taken it out.

Impatient and bored, Talean got up walked in the direction that Eddie went. She walked down the aisle looking on either side of the book stacks. She went down row after row and saw Eddie at the far end of the stacks. He was scanning through a text book. She walked towards him tiptoeing. As she came close he looked up She smiled. "You found it?" she asked

"No man, that book was gone. I am looking for a substitute" he told her

"You sure there was only one copy of it?"

"Well, may be there was another copy, but there was none on the shelf. I have gone through this lot, and I could not find it.

"Alright, I will help you look for the book. Women were more careful in looking out for things." She ran her finger through the bottom shelf, one book at a time. After a while, she brought out a black book with a scruffy look. "Is this it?" she asked him in a low voice.

"Ah! there you are. That is the book. Where did you find it? There pointing to the bottom shelf.

"You have cat eyes to find it, you know. I thought it had been borrowed." He said in a relieved voice

"You were not looking properly. You were thinking about me and not concentrating on what you were doing. Say yes, your mind was not on what you were doing" she said amid laughter.

"Well, not really. I was concentrating on what I was doing; but some one put it there because it was in the wrong shelf. Sometimes some people would hide books that they wanted to use by placing them in the wrong index so that no one will find them, and they would have the exclusive use of that book."

She brushed her index finger over his lips. "You did not want to destroy your pride" she said with a big smile.

Eddie seized the finger, with his lips, sucked it, as he looked at her eye to eye.

She rolled her eyes passionately. "What are you doing?" she asked as she pulled her hand away. "Let go, we were in the library, you know. Stop being silly" she used her left hand to push his head away.

He let go the finger. "I could not keep it in my mouth for ever."

No not in here silly burger. You liked playing like kiddies aren't you?"

"I liked sucking fingers, breasts and all those things."

You never suck your mom's breast? She asked

"I did, but I never had enough of it I still liked it especially when you are.. you get what I mean?

"Shut up now" she told him in a sharp voice as they went down the stairs to the check out desk. "I would buy you a dome" she whispered into his ears. They walked in silence to the issue desk. He placed the book with his library card on the desk.

"You taking them out?" the lady behind the desk asked.

"Yes, please" Talean answered. Eddie was looking away trying to catch Obusah's eye by the photocopier.

He turned round quickly and repeated "yes please" then looked at Talean. She looked at him with apprehension. They walked in silence through the barriers and out into the foyer.

The end of another day" Eddie said, as they walked out through the glass doors to the pavement.

"You did not always concentrate on what you were doing, do for me" she told him

"No man, I do, honest. I would spend a whole day doing what you want. I did not need to tell her that I needed those books. She should sauce that out without me saying it."

"She asked you and you did not bother to answer."

"Oh forget it. It's not worth talking about. Lets talk about what we were going to cook and how. We were going to spend the afternoon together.aren't we?" He asked.

I don't know" she said in a soft voice as she walked behind him. "Why can't we walk together?" she asked.

I am a woman, you know I can't walk that fast. I am not used to walking very fast."

"Oh, I am sorry" he said. He stopped, turned round towards her and smiled and raised his left hand and flung it round her neck. She came close to him. "You did not have to hurry home. We have all afternoon to ourselves. I always have to double my steps to keep up with you. You were more or less running all the time. I got breathless every time I walked with you.

They walked down the road passed the school, and down to the bank. There was a long queue by the cash point at the bank. One lady ran passed then from the cash point. Talean pushed backwards and her bag behind her to make way for the lady. She smelled awful she said to Eddie. He looked at the lady for a while," did she?" he asked. He turned round again to look at the lady who had now crossed the road to the other side. Her black stripped skirt was sticking between her fat legs, making a flip flop sound She walked along in a hurry making the noise as she went

"May be she had been cooking curry and left the flat with out having changed her dress. "Talean said.

"Well, not every body had time to change for every occasion" he replied.

"But you should change your kitchen clothes before you went out." she said defiantly.

"That was true. You would remember to do that but some people never bothered. He put his hand before her, and then held her left hand as the traffic streamed passed them. She turned round; wow we are now surrounded by a small crowd waiting to cross the busy road. The crowd moved forward as the cars stopped on the red light. Eddie and Talean went with them. But Talean's left foot came off the shoe, as she tried to rush with the rest. She bent over to make it. Eddie did not know what had happened and just moved on without looking back and waiting for her to fix her shoe. He got to the other side of the road, while Talean was still in the central reservation. He stood watching her and the traffic moving at high speed. She looked away, as he tried to talk to her. She then walked slowly across with her mouth squeezed into a small nut with an upset face, and avoiding eye contact with him.

He stretched his left hand to receive her on the pavement, but she avoided him and walked on.

'I am sorry, I left you behind. I thought you were in the pack crossing the road in a hurry." He said to her as he walked behind her.

"I let go your hand, because my foot slipped out of the shoe. These shoes were not good for running across a busy road. I was trying to get me foot into the shoe, and you just walked on without looking back to see what I was doing. You did not care if I had fallen down and broken my angle" he was upset.

"Look, we have crossed this road a thousand times. It was a busy road anyway. He slipped his left arm round her, as he spoke.

She pushed his arm forcefully, saying in a loud voice "No not with me though. I have not crossed to this side of the road with you before."

"Oh, you women, you got upset quite easily for every little thing, even what a cat would smell and tickle for a play will upset you" he told her.

"No, that is not true; it was not the case here. You should look after me across the road, stupid man. I could not run with high hill shoes. You should know that, you were not an idiot are you?"

"But you let go my hand" he told her. Eddie stopped and looked behind as the bus 61 pulled up behind them.

She was still walking along without lifting her head. "I had to do my shoes, and I needed both hands to do that. You should have looked back to see what I was doing. That was caring for me, but you did not bother, you just walked on.

She turned round to look at his face. Eddie was several feet behind. She lifted her face, rolled her eyes and stamped her left foot in disgust. You see what I mean; he was not even listening to me. I was only talking to myself.

Eddie realized what was happening, he ran quickly to join her. He opened his arms to embrace her.

"No" she said forcefully "just piss off. He forced her into his arms. "I am sorry dear; I was waiting to see if Kofi was on this bus. I asked him to buy some stuff for me at the Bull Ring. They walked on slowly with his arms around her. "You upset, I know. But you got moody quite easily. A big baby you are, soaking for every little thing. My big baby" he said as he fumbled with her blouse.

"Stop digging me, I do not like that" she stopped, looked at him, with angry looks, and her mouth folded firmly inwards. "Do not play with my tittis on the street. You nasty man I will box you face in if you do not stop. Get that into your flipping head now. You left me on the road at the Zebra crossing and you let me walk on alone yet again. You were looking for your girl friend on the bus, were ya? Now you walk on that side, pointing to the grassy path on the other side of the road. I would walk own this side. Do not talk to me; I will not talk to you. I do not want to hear nothing.

They walked in silence for a while, they came to the entrance to Weston road, and Eddie walked close to her, held her right hand. He swung the arm forward, and she looked at him with stern eyes. "Stop being a baby, we are friends aren't we?" he said to her.

"Oh, we forgot to look for the reference book on school effectiveness by Harris" he told her.

She stopped looked at him "I thought you had that book before, I felt that you still had it." she replied.

"No, I had to return it the other day. It was only one week loan right" They walked on, Eddie still holding her hand as he balanced the books on his right hand.

"How come you did not bother look for the book again when you knew that we still needed it?" She said to him

"Guess what I was blinded by excitement. I was just thinking about what we were going to do this afternoon." He replied in an excited voice.

"You naughty little creep you were making excuses now. What things are you thinking about?" She asked in a curious voice.

"Well we would cook, eat and do some studies. That was it." he said to her.

"You sure that was all you thinking about. What else creepy young man?" she pulled him towards her.

Eddie was looking at the Lloyds bank cricket ground on the other side of the road. "Nothing else really, I just felt excited about being with you and having dinner together"

"But we have been together before haven't we? So what was the big deal." She stretched her hand forward to tell him to move on. Reluctantly, he turned round and walked on slowly. She waited for him to move a few feet. She stood still, both her hands resting on her bag. She then walked passed him. He doubled his steps, caught up with her as they turned into Oakfield road.

"Here we go again, big baby" he teased her. She walked on without saying a word. He put his right hand into his pocket, took out a bunch of keys. He dropped the keys into her hand, saying "you open the door." She stopped, looked at him. "Why me?" she asked. "I did not live here, besides I did not know which was the right key. I am not doing it" she told him. She held the keys between her index finger and thumb swinging them. She pushed her hand into his face. He pulled his head back..

"Oh please open the door." He ran towards the door, she followed him. He turn round with his back against the wall. She flung herself forward with her hands still in the air when he pulled her close to him, squeezed her on his chest. He looked into her eyes. She smiled, and then put her hand on his throat. "No" she said, as she pulled herself away. She walked towards the door, when it suddenly opened. A lady walked out. "Thank you" she said. "There you are" he said to her.

"I did not open it. The lady did. You had me say thank you to her didn't you.

Eddie walked in first. She followed behind. They went to the stairs. Every step was followed by echoes of rocking sound. These were very old stair cases" she said as she took her time to go up. The stairs seemed to be giving way as she walked slowly upwards. She tried to support her weight on the wooden rail. That rail was not strong enough" he told her. "I could see that " she replied. "This was a bit dangerous.

They got to the landing, and turn right into Eddie's room. "You room was just on the landing. He took out the keys again, opened the door, and held it for her to go in first. "No you go in first, it's your room" she told him. He walked in and she stood there for a few seconds, looking round. The wooden stairs to the next floor looked like an abandoned building. They were dark brown with dirt and the carpet stained with dirt like it has been there for hundreds of years. She tuned to look at the aisle at the bottom of the stairs. A lady walked passed quickly. She tried to follow her with her eyes, and she heard a sound of foot steps coming down the next stair case. She realized that only one person at a time, cloud walk on the narrow stair case.

She walked quickly into the room, almost falling into Eddie's arm. "Bops" he said, as his face was just a few inches from hers, and her breast almost touched his.

"I did not realize you were coming out." she told him.

"I was going out to fetch you." he replied.

"I was just having a look round the hall way and stairs. I was admiring at the splendor of the building"

"You being funny aren't you. There was nothing to admire about this building. Its old, neglected and falling apart and only us foreign students and black people for that matter would be put in a building like this.

"No not really, it's a good building, I suppose. Although it needs some attention especially the stairs were a bit rocky.

I tell you what; someone was going to go through those, pointing to the two loose boards near the ground floor, sooner rather than later. And that was just the tip of the ice berg. The stuff in the kitchen was worst than what you have seen so far.

Eddie and Talean were now in Eddie's room. "You have a nice room" she said, as she stood in the middle of the room. She passed her eyes round the room. The small table full of books and files. A book shelf just above the table; full of big and chunky books neatly arranged on both shelves. Eddie sank into the bed. He took the shoes off. He then got up drew the chair, "sit down please"

"Oh, thank you." She continued to look around. She put her bag on the table, sat down, crossed her legs and relaxed in the chair.

Eddie opened the closet, and then came to her "may I hang your jumper in the closet."

"Oh yes, thank you" she said. She took it off and gave it to him. He brought a pair of slippers and gave them to her. "You needed these for the kitchen" he told her.

"You are a good man aren't you? I needed to get out of these shoes; they were a pain in my ass. I wear them only on special occasion like today"

"Today was a special day of course." He said to her. He took the black shoes to the closet. He looked at them admirably with a smiling face. She looked at him, smiled, but did not say a word. She was pleased that he liked her shoes and treated them with respect.

They both changed to go into the kitchen. "Come let us go down to the kitchen" he told her as he opened the door. Eddie was looking forward to spending the afternoon and evening with Talean. Cook and drink and all them things" he said a loud in an exciting voice. "You get what I mean" he looked at her.

She looked at her dress in the mirror. She Talean pulled her dress, Eddie looked with amazement. He was steering at her. "Stop steering at me please. You can never get beyond this space. She put her right hand one foot away from her face down her breast and legs. Nobody gets into this space," she opened her eyes wide. "Don't even think about it, I would not let you" she told him in a soft but determined voice.

"She did not really mean it" he told himself. "Women sometimes say such things in public when in fact they were hiding the truth.

She would give in with just a little pressure and persuasion. He looked at her with cold eyes. "I did not really mean anything wrong" he told her. All I would really need after eating a good dinner was your lips. Your soft and pliable lips, he leaked his lips, stick out his tongue.

She looked at him with cool eyes. 'Are they really soft?" she asked with a broad smile. She stuck out her tongue as an invitation. He nodded repeatedly, and then looked at her inside the eye.

"You sure you would not ask for anything else, after I give you a kiss?" she asked as she come close to him almost brushing her breast on his lips.

"Yea man honest, nothing more" he replied in a slow voice and with a false smile.

"Sure, sure? " looking into his eyes once more. She was not convinced of the reply. "Well, I would not let you anyway, even if you asked.' She said as she walked away.

Eddie laughed, pulled his legs together, and scratched the back of his head, then said "You have my word for it.

She folded her hands across her chest, sat down and pulled her legs together; put her left leg over her right.

"I trust you, you will not rape me" she told him in a soft voice.

"Rape" he repeated. "Please do not mention that word here. I have never, and will never ever do that to a woman." His voice sounded angry and his face changed.

"Please do not take offense. It's just a thought. You were an honest man. A real darling, I knew that" she told him in a reassuring voice. She stood in the middle of the room for a while, looked round. "You have a nice room" she said, as she continued to look round.

"Thank you it's small though, but enough for a bachelor and a book worm." She looked at him with out saying a word. She turned round to look at the small table full of books and files. The book shelf just above the table was neatly packed with big and chunky books.

Eddie sank into the bed, took off his shoes. He got up drew out the chair. "Sit down please" he told her.

"Oh thank you" she put her bag on the table and then sat down and continued to look around. She crossed her legs, and then relaxed in the chair. She watched Eddie changed his clothes.

He opened the closet, put his shoes and shirt. He came up to her "May I hang your jumper in the closet?"

"Oh yes, thank you" she took it off and gave it to him. He brought out a pair of slippers and gave them to her. "You needed these for the kitchen" he told her.

"You are good man, aren't you? I needed to get out of these shoes; they are killing me with pain in my ass. I wear them only on special occasions." She said.

"Today was a special day for us wasn't it? He replied.

"Well, sort of" she replied. "Off course it was. Today was a special day" he said as he took the high hill shoes to the closet. He looked at them admirably with a smiling face.

She looked at him, smiled but said nothing. She was pleased that he liked her shoes and taken them with respect.

"Come on let us go down to the kitchen" he told her.

They both got up, he led the way out of the door, down the stairs case across the dinning hall. "Come in" he said as she hesitated to enter the kitchen. She stood at the door, supporting herself with her left hand, pushing herself. She spotted two ladies both in their thirties, gossiping at the far corner of the kitchen. They both turned round, looked at Talean. She smiled, the ladies smiled back. "Hi" the lady in the multi colored African dress said. "Do not hesitate; there are a few of us here with these men, rubbing shoulders together every day. He is a good guy" pointing to Eddie. "He is very friendly and hard working too.'

"He could cook as well" added the other lady, in a pink long dress, big earring and her head neatly tied up, covering her ears. Talean looked at Eddie with a big smile, and then said I hope you were not trying to make him feel proud. He could not cook better than a woman. Not me anyway" sticking her index finger on her chest.

Eddie now full of air of importance was rubbing his hands together with a broad smile on his face. He walked as if he was on quick sand.

We watched these men each day cooking their meals. You could tell if someone was cooking a good meal. Some of these men could not really cook. Honest. He was the exception. His friends were learning from him by watching him cook." The lady said.

"Well, the test of the pudding is in the eating isn't it? I am here to taste his cooking today. By the way my name is Talean." She moved forward to shake hands with the two ladies.

Rubina, Hawanatu.

"You are West Indian?" asked Rubina.

"Yes. I am" replied Talean.

I could tell from your accent.

"Eddie and I are doing the same course at the University.

We are at the University as well. I am in the English faculty and Hawanatu is in Social Studies.

"Time to start cooking" Eddie told Talean. "What do you want to eat?" He asked.

"You just cook your favorite meal man" she told him.

You will eat anything I cook?"

Yea man, I am a stranger, you just eat what was provided. Besides I wanted to eat typical African food today."

That was easy then" he said. "Rice and stew. He opened his food cupboard, took out rice, tomato. You could go and watch telly in the room or in the hall." He told her.

"Nooo" she replied. I would stay with you. I would like to watch you do the cooking.

Hmmm! It's a nice dinner. I enjoy it. I was a bit peckish. I tried not to eat anything while I was waiting for this. The ladies were right, you could cook. Let me do the washing up for you, please. She got up took the plates to the sink, opened the tap. I would do it. You just relax. I am here to serve you. When I came to yours, it would be your turn to serve me. Talean looked at him with disappointing eyes, and then stepped aside. He threw a tea towel at her. "Wipe your hands" he told her.

"Oh gush, I had more food than I should have had. I am feeling a bit of pain in my Tommy" Talean said, as she balanced her weight on her left leg. She had her left hand on the table, still balancing on the chair. "The dinner was so nice that I couldn't stop eating.

CHAPTER 23

▼

Eddie sat on the edge of the bed with both hands on the bed to support his weight. Talean looked a bit uncomfortable. "You should have just had you usual ration.

"I did not want to waste your food "she replied.

"Bloody hell, I would not eat more than what I could, to please anyone.

"Be a gentleman!" she said in a deep voice, as she turned round to look at him.

"I am sorry" he said and he got up. "Should we get on with some thing like working on our essays?"

"Oh yes, lets discuss that assignment for Mr. Mercer. I did not quite understand it. I would not be a minute; I am going to get another chair from the hall. He shut the door behind him.

Talean watched the door closed. She got up, looked inside each draw. As she walked to the closet, she saw her self on the mirror. She went closer to have a close look at her face. "Oh my make up was all gone. My mouth had no more lipstick. She danced round, "My bum was sticking out" she said. She then felt her breast.

This titti was itching all the time. Let me change this dress I am hot in it." She took a packet from her bag, unwrap it, put it on the bed. She took off her dress, looked at her body in the mirror. She danced round again to have a good look at her shape. She then combed her hair, tied it into a nut, passed her finger over her eye brows. She then checked her cheeks and lips. She weighed her breasts, then took out her right breast examined it, chucked it back. She watched her bum again and her thighs. She ran her palm through her thighs, feeling the smooth and even texture of the skin. She took the pink dress, examined it at arms length, before slipping it in. She took her lipstick from the bag when the door opened. She dropped it back and sat down quickly. She put her hand inside her bag and if she was searching for something in it.

"You look beautiful in this dress. This was not what you had on earlier was it?" he asked.

"Oh well, I just decided to change into this one. This was an evening dress.

I Felt more relaxed in it. I wanted to be relaxed and breathed more comfortably" she said in a low soft voice. "You see, when you were going out, you wear clothes that made your shape look nice. So we have dressed for going out and dressed for indoors.

This dress was for indoors only. I would not think of wearing it to go places. No never. But you liked me in it don't you?" She surveyed her self in the dress.

"I would write out that essay, so that you do not have to worry about it, or have to do it your self." he told her.

"That was alright then" she replied in a condescending voice. "But what would I be doing. I thought we were going to read together the chapter on effective administration?

"You read; I listen. Do you mind? She asked.

"No, not at all I like reading" he replied.

"I love to be entertained." she told him in a laughing voice.

Eddie glanced at his book shelf; he took out a thick gray book. He went back and sat on the bed.

"You were going to start reading now? What an efficient man you are. Well, we might as well get on with it right away. Do you mind if I lie down on your bed and listen while you read" She asked.

"You were welcome" he replied, pointing her to the bed.

"Very kind of you sir, You have given me food, now you have given me your bed to relax." She got up from the chair walked to the bed. She hesitated to sit at first, looked at Eddie who was busy turning the pages of the book. He pretended not to notice her.

She sat down first, and then lay on her back. She got up quickly; put her right hand over her mouth.

Eddie turned round, "You ok" What was the matter" he asked.

"Nothing" she replied in a faint voice. "I just thought it was wrong to lie in your bed" she added in a soft and unsure voice

"Flipping heck, nothing was wrong about it. I am not a ghost, am I?"

She shook her head, looked at him with guilty eyes.

"You are in good hands, just relax; I got the message, I would take you home safely in one piece." He told her in a sharp voice.

"You sure" she change her voice into a lovely and strong tone, may be he was right she thought. Nothing would happen; she heard a voice telling her. She lay back, first on her back, then on her left side with her face to the wall.

He read for a while, and then turned round to see if she was listening. She was still and her eyes closed. He closed the book, and went out quietly. He came back with two cans of skol beer. He opened the door quietly, but it made a screeching noise. She woke up, looked round, and saw Eddie by the door with the two cans.

"Where have you been? I thought you were reading to me" she questioned.

"You were not listening. Would you like a drink? He lifted one can up in the air.

She hesitated first, and then said "Yes please. I would have a little bit. But why did you stop reading and walked away?"

"It was simply because you were sleeping" He dragged the letters of the last word into a melody, as he handed her the can. "You were fast asleep minutes after I started reading.

"Was I?" she asked in a surprised voice. She got up; sat down, put her fingers into her mouth. "I am sorry, I felt a bit tired. Your bed was comfortable you know

"Alright, drink your beer. I would sit by you and read again" he told her.

"Sit by me, where? " She asked, putting her hand on her chest.

Eddie took a sip of the beer "On the side of the bed off course. You lie down" he looked at her.

She rolled her eyes up, then closed them and put her hand over her face. What was going on here? She asked herself. Some men were crafty and could be naughty.

He pulled her hand away from her face. "You would be OK, lady. You did not need any prayers for your safety in my room, trust me. He took another sip of his beer.

I was thinking about something actually. She opened the can, took a sip of beer. She pulled herself up to the headboard, rested on it, took another sip of the beer. She had the can on the right hand, resting on her thigh.

Eddie took the book again and started reading. He read two pages, looked at her. "You were not listening, were you?" he asked.

"Yes, I am" she replied. Go on man, my ears were wide open"

Eddie bent over the book, read two paragraphs.

"Excuse me please." She pushed herself out of the bed, got up. She put the can on the table, and went to the window. She looked across the street.

"Anything exciting out there? He asked, as he got up and joined her by the window. The book was still in his left hand. He looked down the street, turned round and put the book on the table face down. He moved closer to her .They were both looking down the street, as he edged closer to her slowly. He put his right hand on her shoulder, and then slipped it slowly down her right breast.

"What are you doing? She asked in an angry voice.

I am trying to look down the street as well" he replied.

She turned round, looked into his eyes with angry looks.

He smiled. She folded her mouth inwards and then smiled.

He pulled her closer, but she tried to free herself. "Please don't" she said in a frightened voice. He wrapped his hands round her. She jacked her head backwards; turned her head left to right. She looked into his eyes; she felt a chilling sensation down her body. She closed her eyes, and then relaxed her body. She dropped her head down on his shoulder.

It was the minute Angel Gabriel had been waiting for. The hour of passion took over. There was dead silence, except the clicking away of the minutes by the clock. The minutes rolled fast without notice. The firm grip and tender caressing went on and on. Not even the noise of a fire alarm could have been taken notice of. Like hungry lions, the wet kisses were pouring saliva down the cheeks unnoticed. The warm tender glue and the squeezing of arms round each other was all that matters.

When he let go, she looked around "where am I?" she asked. "Its like I was drowning, honest" She open her mouth, stuck her tongue out. Eddie seized it again like a hungry lion, gobbling his feast.

When Talean woke up later, it was already dark. She looked like a drunkard coming out from a deep sleep. She looked round" what time is it?

She asked in a slewed voice.

"Oh gush, I should be going home now." She pushed the bed covers quickly, got up in a hurry, dressed up quickly.

She walked to the door, after a quick glance at the mirror. "Where were you going?" Eddie asked still in bed.

"To the toilet" she replied. She turned round, went to the mirror by the closet door. "I thought you were going to the toilet. I would save it until I get home."

"You were saving it for one hour bus ride home?" he asked in a sarcastic voice.

I am not desperate. It would wait, get up and get dressed. I wanted to get on the next bus to town.

Eddie got up, stretched himself. "I would be back in a second he dashed to the toilet.

Alone in the room again, she surveyed her face, hair and dress. She put on her lipstick and makeup on.

Eddie came back into the room. I would be ready in five minutes" he told her.

As she buried her face on his chest, she murmured. "This had been the best day I have had for ages."

"You lips are so soft and pliable" he told her as he kissed her good bye. I will see you on your bus in the city center." he told her. I am coming with you to town.

"I have had a real good time, thank you for everything" she gave him a peck on the left cheek. She walked out of the room. They walked up the road to Bristol Street to wait for the bus to the city

"Hurry up, here is the bus. " She told him as they crossed the road to the bus stop. She got on the bus, stood at the door waiting for Eddie. They went upstairs and sat at the front seat, her left hand on Eddie's lap.

There was my bus" she told him as the bus pulled up at Colmore Road bus station in the city center. I do not want to miss that bus. We better rush out quick. I would see you at the day center tomorrow. Talean rushed and got on Bus 74. The bus driver closed the door. She sat down, blew him a kiss and the bus moved away. Eddie waited until the bus went round the corner and disappeared. He was still looking at the direction of bus 74, when his bus pulled up. He turned round and saw the last passenger bus pulling out. He ran quickly and got on it.

CHAPTER 24

▼

It was late in the evening when Talean got home. Shed went into the kitchen to make a cup of tea. She was singing and dancing while making the tea.

"You were really happy today weren't you?" her aunt said as she came into the kitchen. She opened the fridge, took out some sweets "the day must have been exciting for you wasn't it?" She left without waiting for a reply. Talean was watched by her aunt, but said nothing. She realized that her aunt was still watching her from the landing. She turned round looked at her aunt, smiled, then said "well, sort of. I was with my college mates. We cooked eat and we were just talking about all sorts of things. You get what I mean? There was nothing out of the ordinary actually. One funny man joined our conversation. He made us laugh all the time. I could not stop laughing. I got a Tommy ache in the end. I have never met so funny a man."

She went to the living room, sat down and watched the telly with her aunt and uncle for a while. She jacked herself suddenly, tipping her cup of tea on the carpet. "Oh dear me" she mourned. "I have made a mess here. Mr. and Mrs. Howard turned and looked at what she had done. They exchanged glances and went back to watching the telly "Your mind was not in this house today" her aunt said.

"Oh, it's just an accident I did not mean to spill the tea on the carpet I will clean it up anyway. She got up, went into the kitchen, came back with the Hoover and mopped the floor. She went back into the kitchen to put back the Hoover. "I am going to my bed. Good night" she said and hurried up the stairs into her bedroom.

It was early in the morning next day when Talean left the house for work. Her aunt and Uncle were still in bed when she left to catch the early bus to Handsworth.

She got to the day care center early enough, thinking she was the first one to get there. The lights were on and she could hear the noise of the kids.

Good morning Ms Talean. You are very early today" said Faye. She smiled, looked round the small hall. There were only four children sitting on the carpet. Faye was already putting together the triangular tables for the children's morning tea.

Talean put her Portfolio near the foot of the stairs, went to help Faye lay the tables.

Morning Ms T. said a parent in her twenties with three children. One was in the bogie, the second one about three hanging on her scat. "Go and sit on the carpet" she told the older girl who was about five years old. "Ms T. could I have a word with you please" the mother said as she pushed the bogie out of the way. Her daughter reluctantly went to sit down, rubbing her eyes and sobbing quietly. "If you do not shut up, I would give you a big smack before I leave. Nasty little thing" she said in an angry voice.

"Has she been naughty at home? Talean asked smiling; she stretched both arms to receive the little girl and comforted her.

"She was getting ever so naughty. She got on my nerves all the time now. She would not eat her dinner and she got temper tantrums often. I hardly believed what she is getting up to." She came close to Talean. "What I wanted to talk you about was that I am going to Coventry, and I might not make it back on time to pick her up at 3.30. But I would try to be here shortly after that. Would that be all right?" she asked in a polite voice.

Talean looked up at Helen. "You were not taking them two with you are you?" she asked, pointing to the little girl in the Bogie and the other little girl who had her face behind her moms scat.

"No, I am leaving them with my friend. This one has slight fever, pointing to the baby in the Bogie who just sneezed out lots of snought. "But I have to make the trip. Its important that I went this morning" she replied.

"Well, it should not be a problem, as long as you get here before 4.30 pm." Talean assured her.

"Oh yes, I should be here long before that time. Thanks ever so much." She turned round, wheeled the Bogie and left. Talean held the door for her, as she struggled to get the Bogie out into the foyer, then to the pavement. Talean waved her with a smile. She continued to hold the door open for the parent coming in with her son.

"Good morning Ms Hill. Could I have a word with you? I needed to talk to you, it's urgent" said the parent as she walked through the door. She took off the Anorak in a hurry from her son, rushed to hang it.

"Good morning Soffie," Talean replied. "You could talk to me of course. Is it private? Shall we go up to the office or out in the foyer.

"What ever" she replied. Her voice was subdued and moody. She pushed the child toward the carpet.

Sofia went into the hall and walked toward the stairs. Talean took her portfolio from the stairs and followed Sofia up the stairs.

"I liked that you know to be more private and personal" Talean told Soffie as she walked behind. Talean now at the foot of the stairs hurried passed the hall.

Sofia now in a smiling mode walked passed Talean. She waved to Faye and the children. The children all seated and having breakfast of biscuits and a cup of milk.

The children all answered in a chorus bye, some waving back.

Rueben's mum" said the boy next to him. "Did your mum have a boyfriend? asked the girl opposite Rueben. "My mum has. He came to our house every day, he sold marijuana" said the girl. "Is he a Rastafara?" Rueben asked. The girl nodded.

"My dad was a Rasta, but he did not sell drugs" Rueben said as he ate the last biscuit.

"But he sniffed drugs doesn't he? Rueben nodded. My mum smokes drugs as well' he added.

"Shut up and eat your food." Faye shouted. No more of that she went on Line up for the toilet. Talean shouted. No talking she added.

Faye, you clear the tables and pack them. I would do the toileting and then wash up the cups and spoons afterwards, while you read a story to them. Tobias and Tamika go in first. Remember to do a wee, wash your hands and dry them with the paper towel and go straight to the carpet.

Faye sat on the low chair in front of the children. She held a bright colored book. "Shut up and listen. Aduke turn round and listen. Michael move and sit here near me," pointing to an empty space near her. If you could not sit near Natalie, then you sit alone.

I will read the story, and then you go out to play. Who did not like Mrs. Red Riding Hood.

Michelle shut her hand up" I do not like that book. "I do not like it said Danielle.

Faye put the book back on the shelf and took another book. "Who does not like this book?" she asked.

"Mee " in chorus the children answered.

"Which one do you like then?" she asked again.

Woonie the pooh shouted Rueben. "Do you all like Woonie the Pooh?

"Yes" they all answered. Faye got up went to the bookshelf to get the book.

All the children ran out into the play ground. The play ground had only one slide, a trampoline and one climbing frame. The children ran in all directions, using every available space and equipment. The four staff and two helpers were all outside to supervise the free play period. Talean went to help. She helped the children struggling to climb on the slide.

"Jennifer, I am going to college after dinner. You were staying late today aren't you, yes, I am" she came close to Talean as she pushed Tobias on the tricycle.

CHAPTER 25

▼

It was early morning. Eddie got up as usual to avoid the rush into the toilet. He stretched himself, then looked round, and then through the window. It was quiet and still outside, with a gentle breeze. He opened the door, went to the toilet. Obusah was pushing the door from the inside to lock it, while Eddie was pulling to open. The door jacked forward and hit Obusah on the forehead. "Bops" he shouted. "What the hell?" Eddie's towel round his neck fell.

"How are you sir, chief of the international house" Obusah said jokingly.

Without saying a word, Eddie bent over, picked his towel.

"You are real king among the cronies in the house.

John was coming down the stairs to the toilet. "John" the chief was here, solute him please. Obusah walked back into the toilet, followed by Eddie and john. John shut the door behind him. Eddie moved over to the second wash hand basin. John turned round, the toothbrush still in his mouth. He put his right hand under his Tommy; and his left hand behind his back. He bowed down before Eddie. I solute your highness.

"Fuck off before me" Eddie said as he sucked his teeth, ignoring john.

I solute your highness sir

He bowed the second time stretched his right hand.

"Please do not start, it's too early" said Eddie as he washed his mouth.

"You are the greatest man in the whole of the manor" Obusah opened the door, walked out, then came back pushed his head inside and said "he was vaginated last night." he shut the door quickly before Eddie spat out the tooth paste from his mouth. "You shut up" Eddie said, but Obusah had already gone he turned round but Obusah had disappeared. He went back into his room.

Eddie dressed up quickly and went down to the kitchen. He put his book on the table in the dinning hall, he went into the kitchen to make breakfast. He opened his food cupboard to get the sugar and cornflakes out when he heard foot steps behind him. He turned round.

"Good morning Eddie" Sahida said smiling and her sweet perfume quickly over whelmed Eddie. "Where is your friend?" she asked. He was bemused, but not surprised. He smiled back. "This was the best entertainment I have had for a long time; a beautiful woman in so nice a dress and a nose raising odor. How are you. I did not get your question Miss.

Which friend? He asked in a soft voice. He put back the sugar. He took the plate, held it for a short while, and then put it back on the table. He looked at the lady in the eye.

"I meant your friend yesterday. Her name was Talean she told me.

"Oh yea, I got you now. He took two steps from the table, and then turned round. "She should be at her work place I guess," he replied in a low voice.

"I thought she was a student?"

"Yes she was both a student, and also worked full time in a day care center far away from here."

"Oh you mean she work and study at the same time?" she asked.

"She worked and study part time" he repeated.

Sahida shifted her weight from left to the right foot. She was a nice woman; I liked her. Some women were so proud that they would not talk to any other woman. She had smiles all over her face and she loved chatting you know.

She was not a chatter box you know "Eddie assured her; she only talk to people she felt confident with.

But I am a stranger. We never met before. You get what I mean? And yet she had a good conversation with me. How did you come to know her if I may ask?" Sahida moved closer to Eddie. She put her two hands on the table. Eddie pushed the plate to the far end of the table, moved back to face Sahida.

"She was my class mate, we were doing the same course and we worked together in our assignments and reports. They put us together, simply because we happened to sit close together on the day the professor gave out the first group work. We have been together ever since, doing our group work" he told her in a calm and confident voice.

"You were very lucky to be paired with so beautiful and pleasant woman She was into you I could guess that. You liked her don't you?" she asked looking into his eyes with a smile. She jacked her head forward to guage his reaction. His facial expression did not reveal anything, not even yesterdays events.

"Well" he exclaimed. He twisted his face to show signs of indifference. He did not want to share out his secret admiration for Talean, which he had cherished from the moment he saw her in the reception. The quick contest he won after the reception, by acompanying her to the bus stop in favor of the other contestant.

She was a nice woman, and approachable" he told her. You could talk to her just about subject" he went on. She was intelligent too and had lots of experience about things.

"That was not what I wanted to know. I asked you a question. You have not answered it." She moved one step to the right, rested her back on the table and stood directly in front of Eddie. She folded her arms across her chest, then rested them behind her back on the table.

Eddie first felt like a child been squeezed by his mum for information. He felt chills going down his spine. Then as her aroma went down his throat, he said to himself. "Oh gush, may be a kiss was what she was asking for. He straightened himself up, he then realized that his fore head was only inches away from her small molded nose and thin succulent lips. She remained motionless, as fantasies crept across Eddie's mind. He seized the opportunity of piercing into her eyes. Her twinkling eyes shown behind her round smooth face like distant stars. They gave Eddie a slight gnaw under his Tommy. His heart was pounding like a little tom tom. She smiled as he breath in her ebony deodorant. Eddie was transfixed. She could guess what was going through Eddie's mind, but she remained passive, motionless and hypnotized, as he stood over her like a hungry loin watching over its meal. He was petrified, and could not say a word, not even the answer to her question, which he must have forgotten any way. Eddie smiled again.

And suddenly from no where the voice like thunder in a March month "Oh ho; what was going on here" a voice came from behind the main door to the kitchen. They both turned round suddenly to see who it was.

"Eddie! you again?" John asked in a rather unusual voice, as he entered the kitchen

Sahida stretched her arms and push Eddie from her personal space she walked quickly passed John, avoiding an eye contact, and any sign of noisiness.

In came Renee and she watched Eddie doubling his steps backwards from Sahida's push from her personal space. "This was the man I wanted to see." But she stopped for a second to watch what was going on.

Sahida's hands were still on Eddie's Tommy and his fingers locked into Sahida, as he tried to pull her hands off himself.

"What were you two doing in the kitchen this early morning. This was the wrong place for that sort of play." She walked to them. "What were you trying to do to Eddie?" she asked Sahida in a joking voice as she tried to intervene.

"You liar" Eddie said in a soft voice. "It's all your fault" he said as he pushed his face forward to her.

"My fault? Fuck you. Your nose was just inches away from my lips. I was edging out and trying to back away from you and you kept coming forward.

"Never mind" said Renee. "He was a nice guy anyway. Any woman would love to kiss your lips" said Renee, as she put her index finger on his lips. She then turned round sharply to Sahida, looked into her eyes.

"What a daring man you were, that was naughty you know." Renee said in a stern voice with her lips tightened. "You have all these beautiful women right under your nose. You went out miles away from this compound to look for a woman and you have the gut to bring her into our kitchen" She tightened her teeth as she said the word kitchen. 'You did not fancy any one here, did you? What did she posses that none of us have? A stray he goat you are" her voice was getting more croaky.

"He does not look under his nose, he looks over his nose. Silly bastard" she said as she struck her index finger on his lips

"I asked him a question, he did not answer it yet, he preferred to admire my face. He never admired it before until today. What an idiot you are. You have sleepy brains that needed to be screwed up before you wake up" said Sahida.

"Do you like Sahida?" Renee asked him.

Eddie smiled, looked at Sahida. He then rubbed his hands together. "That was an open invitation, you know." he replied forcefully. "No woman would let you into her personal space if she was not interested in you.

"No you wrong, definitely wrong" Sahida stormed in an angry voice." I was not inviting you. I was talking to you, and it happened that I was just standing too close to you. That was not an invitation for you to have a kiss of me.

"Your spongy lips were too inviting. No man would resist that temptation. Honest.

She was married, you know

"But a little kiss would not draw blood out of stones, would it?" he said jokingly.

"You should not kiss another man's wife. Creepy little man, you should not. Get that into your flipping head" Renee told him.

And so what" he said in an out burst.

Renee pushed her head close to his, open her eyes wide" do not try it again. Full stop. You understand that. Get that into your head straight away. Eddie looked into Renee's eyes. She stuck her tongue out at him.

"How do you know that she was married anyway?"

Its easy to guess that" she replied. The two women stood with their backs against the table, facing Eddie.

Eddie looked round, and then looked at Renee, then Sahida and his watch.

You were not leaving this building just yet were you? Renee asked him.

I would leave in a bit." He replied. He turned the strap of his watch, balanced his weight from left to right.

Renee's hands were on her hips, while Sahida's were still folded across her chest.

John came into the kitchen and walked straight into the conversation. The ladies exchanged glances and walked away without another word.

"Hey, why were you leaving." He watched then for a few seconds and then turned to Eddie "You were a great guy. These girls don't talk to any one. They were so proud that, not every one admired their beauty. I certainly don't although dirty water could put out blazing inferno.

"But these are not dirty water by any means. Both of them were nice women" Eddie insisted. You have to accept that fact.

"But why don't they want to talk to anyone?" John asked in an angry voice.

"Look here" Eddie held John by the shoulder. "All women were like that, you know. You have to talk to them. Sometimes you have to force a conversation with them. You get what I mean?. They were always shy. Sometimes they were not sure of what to say and they would not trust you until they get to know you. Sometimes you wanted to talk to them, they ignored you or simply walked away.

John sucked his teeth and frown. "That was exactly what I hated, I didn't like been ignored" he said in a forceful voice, and demonstrating with his hands emphasizing his point of view.

Eddie held him on the shoulders with both hands. "You listen to me, and get this straight into your ears If a woman ignored you, that did not mean that she does not like you. Sometimes she was testing you.

"I did not like to be tested though, because it's preying on the weak part of the man." John told Eddie.

"Would you shut up and listen. I am giving you the rubrics of how to get into a woman mind."

"Alright, go on I am listening" he told Eddie.

I tell you one thing about all the women I have met, and I am of the opinion that the no a woman gave you when you tried to talk to her for the first time did not always come from the bottom of her heart; it's a test of your courage. They hardly come out and tell you their feelings, not this lot anyway.

You were a joker Eddie" John rebuffed him. 'You mean after I have been ignored or told to piss off, I go back crawling after that woman again no way. Eddie turned towards his food cupboard, he took out a mug, held it for a while, then put it back

Obusah came into the kitchen noisely, laughing loudly he did not notice Eddie and John at first. He calmed down a little and then noticed the two men standing near each other. He walked up to them Eddie had his hand over his mouth.

"What were you saying, Eddie turned round to face Obusah. Let us go and sit down." Obusah told them. He led the way into the dinning hall. He walked to the long table; put his plate down and the packet of cornflakes. Eddie and Obusah sat opposite each other.

"I saw you this early morning kissing Sahida in the kitchen, you know" Obusah told Eddie. This was too early man. It was not good timing. You could have waited in your room or hers. That would have been more decent and discrete. This place was too public, defying African tradition. Making a public show was disgusting. Honest. You wanted us to watch didn't you?

Eddie sat quietly eating his cornflakes. He took two spoonful in a row. "You were crazy man; nothing further away from the truth than that do not try to be too economical with the truth in this place, it did not pay anything.

"Hay man, there was only one reason for standing that close to a woman. You get what I mean?"

Eddie looked a bit upset. "Listen folk, I am being honest. It was just a conversation. That was it"

"A conversation only" Obusah repeated in a sarcastic way, "While you invaded her personal space

"Hay Obusah, She had been eyeing him since she came into the dinning hall. I have been watching them ever since. I guess both of them were interested in him. I think.

"So you have not been eating your breakfast then, if you were busy watching them. A creepy young man you must be then" Obusah said laughing.

"No man, I am not. I was just watching their reactions John replied.

Eddie put down his spoon. "He was a real creep, he had time to watch stupid things.

"Well, you call them stupid things. You may be right, but remember that was some one's entire happiness. No one will be quite happy to live alone without the other half of him even for a shot while. Let alone one whole year.

You will get one if you make an effort. Oh yea dam it, it just occurred to me.

"Listen man there would be a party at the TREES pub tonight" Obusah announced. Are you coming Eddie? I am certainly going. It's a men's night.

"Men's night flipping hell, why would you like to watch strippers? Eddie asked in a stranger voice.

"We were going for a drink, then watch the nudes and possibly get one home for a nuke night. added John.

Eddie shuffled his feet, looked right then left. "I am not too sure if I would make it with you guys.

You should come with us. You could help each of us get a partner tonight. There will be lots of them especially white girls. Obusah urged Eddie.

"To hell with him, if he did not come with us he had his nuke treat last night. Besides he was making inroads into these hard to catch fishes of the wild. There will be lots of girls who you do not need a big bait to fish out. Both of us would be bonded tonight. Let him stay with these black women who were making things looked like a real trip to heaven" John said emphatically.

You are wrong" Eddie replied, as he looked at John eye to eye. "I am just talking to them, because they need someone to talk to. Infact they opened up the conversation. I should talk to them naturally. They needed company. You get what I mean?

John looked at Eddie with unconvinced eye. He sucked his teeth, and then cleared his throat. "You have made a pass to Sahida. Haven't you?

No not at all" Eddie shook his head left to right.

"Liar" Obusah shouted. You have already kissed her Don't tell us fips little cheat. I saw you with my own eyes. He turned round and made a sign of the cross.

No man, nonsense that is. I was just talking to her. How could I when she was not my woman.

Leave him alone, he would not tell us the truth" John told Obusah "Let sleeping dogs lie" he went on.

John watched Jenneh walked slowly towards them. She came and stood by Eddie of the table, her back was against the table, facing the opposite direction She avoided Eye contact with Eddie.

Here we go again Shouted Obusah in a strange voice, without lifting his head. Even blind people could bear witness to this.

Jenneh heard him, but pretended not to have heard him. "You were going to the campus this evening? She asked Eddie.

With a mouthful he nodded . He put the spoon down, covered his mouth with his hand for a while.

We would wait for you. You walk with us to the campus OK. She patted his right shoulder, she got up and went to sit by Sahida who came in and sat at the far end table. They exchanged glances smiled and then talk quietly in whispers

John watched with interest at Renee's long dress The multicolored dress dazzled his eyes. As she got up to go, he looked at her chest. He watched her vital figure. A real African beauty, he thought, The spoon dropped from his hand into the plate.

"Are you sleeping? Obusah asked. Poor man, he was admiring the women and had forgotten that he was eating.. You were sowing the seeds of pomposity on these hobos. You were making them feel really proud. She was OK, but by gluing your eyes on them like a dead dog you lifting them up.

CHAPTER 26

▼

It was time to leave, more and more of the student residents came into the dinning hall in a hurry to eat and dash of to the campus. The sitting places were not enough for all the residents. The sooner one finished eating and left the place for another student the better. Obusah had eaten and was waiting to leave, John and Eddie were still eating. The two ladies sat on edge at the other table waiting perhaps for Eddie. The two women took their bags, got up and hung their bags on their shoulders ready to go. They talked in low voices and laughed.

These ladies have got him by the ear clips" Obusah said in a low voice, pointing his mouth at Eddie. Eddie was eating slowly, absent minded and oblivious of his friends sitting by him. His eyes and thoughts seemed to be on the plate, as he ate slowly.

"Shall we wait for you Eddie?" John asked.

"No man, let's go. He had company" Obusah said in a raised voice. "Get up and lets get out of here" he insisted. "Calm down man" John told him. "No need soaking over spilled milk" he went on.

"Spilled milk? He repeated. This was far from it. Its simply black and white.

But you could not force an issue with this lot. We have been here for three months now. If there was anything for a poor man, it would have happened already. So we needed to accept our fate.

You do not know nothing serious. How come all of a sudden, he is getting all the attention in the world? We have all made attempts and pass words, without success. He never made any effort. In fact he once told me that he was not interested."

You were sure about that. How come he was now showing interest in any one of them girls.

Oh yea, you were thinking backwards we were not living in the past. How would you say that he would not have said so? Don't you have eyes to see and a mind to think. Let alone commonsense to read between the lines" Obusah got up forcefully. He took his plate, walked into the kitchen and put it in the cupboard without washing it.

Renee and Sahida came and sat on the table next to the guys. They strained their ears to catch the conversation between the men. He closed the cupboard with such force that it opened again behind him. But he did not look back. The ladies watched through the open door. They went out of the hall quickly.

Eddie looked up and was alone. He got up and went out in a hurry. He met the ladies in the TV room.

Obusah walked passed quickly with angry steps.

John watched with astonishment, but was lost with words. He shook his head with disbelief.

"You upset him John? Renee asked jokingly.

"No I did not" he replied, turning round to face her "I have nothing to do with it; he was upset with himself. He was a coward.

Coward!" she repeated. Men were usually brave. How could he be a coward. He was a smart man wasn't he?

John, the two ladies and Eddie walked out of the door into the side walk to the campus.

"You wanted the truth? John went on. He was jealous of you lot.

Jealous of me, never Eddie said. You liar you were trying to hide the truth.

I am dead serious. Honest He was.

Nonsense that was what were you saying to me he could not bring his wishes out into the open those were idiotic assumptions. She was upset and walked fast ahead of the group. Sahida doubled her steps and joined her. They both walked fast in silence. Eddie doubled his steps and joined them.

John stayed back and walked slowly behind them he could not hear the conversation between them and Eddie.

It was the end of the day. The last lecture had just ended. Eddie and Talean went out. Eddie stretched himself, while Talean yawned, stretched her right arm. "The lecture seemed long and complicated. The details were getting out of hand. Boredom was creeping in the lecture theater. I lost thread of the details" she said quietly. With her mind still wondering Talean was not listening to what the lecturer was saying towards the end of the lecture. I looked blank and stopped taking notes. I had the pen in my mouth, rolling it gently.

I saw that Eddie told her. I knew that you were bored. Talean was exhausted and had a slight headache. "I am not feeling well, you know" she told him. They went and sat on the bench in the foyer. Her elbows rested on her thighs, supporting her head. I am going straight home she told him.

I would have to take you home and come back with the last bus to town.

"No man, I would be alright. I would get home alright for sure.

I am not letting you go alone all that long distance. You looked tired and you have a head ache. Anything could happen on the way. You get what I mean. I am not only saying to you, but I am caring as well.

She looked up at Eddie. Her face had tiny wrinkles. Her cheek muscle all tightened up giving a sad looking face. The nice smooth face had been replaced by a sad looks of an invalid.

You looked really sick" he told her, as he sat besides her. He tried to make her talk, but she was too tired to make a response. I gave my books to Obusah to take them home, and then we would walk down to the bus stop.

Talean was in two minds about Eddie coming home with her. It's an idea" she told herself. I could introduce him to my relatives as a college mate who was helping me with my assignments. But what would my aunt say and think about him?

It might seem daft to them for a stranger to accompany me all the way home. An African for that matter whom they think was an alien and not up to their standard and expectation. These old people do not think much of African people and they might not even want to see him in their house. They might not want to talk to him as most West Indians do. They have told me lots of nasty things about African people. If I went home with him, all that long distant, my Aunt might think that something naughty was going on between us. But I could not just turn down his offer to take me home. That will not be fair and a good behavior on my part. He might be upset, and I enjoyed his company. I am going home with him anyway, and we will have an hour or two together. I did not care what my aunt thinks about him or our relationship as students working together on a common course. I would explain to her she was miserable sometimes but that would be alright.

Obusah came breathing heavily. "What was wrong you ok? John was not in the library. I had to go to the third floor, I could not catch the lift. I came back using the stairs. The lift had to go to the sixth floor, and I could not wait for it. I ran down the stairs.

Sit down and catch your breath. She held his left hand and pulled him down on the bench.

He sat down for a while. Talean suddenly regained her strength and was now feeling alright. She now looked bright and lively.

Get up, let us go to the bus stop. Talean got up and was hopping down the road. She found herself walking ahead of Eddie. She waited for him. "How come I am walking faster than you today. I usually have to double my steps to keep up with you.

You were not alright, you have a head ache and you were tired as well.

I am not too tired to walk though. I would get home alright. I would make you a cup of tea as soon as we got home. Eddie walked behind her. She held his hand pulling him along. They got on the bus "upstairs" she said. They went up the stairs. She looked round, all strange faces. She sat down with her hands between her legs. Eddie turn round nudged her with his elbow. "What were you thinking about? She turned round quickly, smiled "nothing" she replied. I was just enjoying the scenery. The rows of rubber trees made a nice view.

You loved nature. I could guess.

Oh yes, I lived in the country side. Trees and bushes were part of my every day life. These trees reminded me of my village. She took his hand, put it on her lap, and riveted her fingers into his. She looked round then put her fingers into his mouth. She said to herself, I wished I could kiss him, but every one was looking

Get up and let us go down stairs. As they waited for the driver to open the doors she said "my house was just round the corner. Thank you" she said to the driver. They walked in silence for a short while and they came to a semi detached house. She opened the door and she went in first. She put her index finger on his mouth, walked quietly into the sitting room

Good evening Aunty and Uncle. This was Eddie my college mate. I nearly passed out after the lecture. I begged him to accompany me home. I thought I might not make it home.

That was very kind of him. What happened to you? asked Mr. Wright

I was very tired and I had headache as well. I had a bad day at the day care center. I went with the headache actually, and it got worst at the end of the day.

Were you alright now that you were home? Mrs. Wright sat in a reclining chair, her glasses were just at the tip of her nose Mr. Wright was lying on the sofa.

I am not really alright, my head still hurts. I am just trying to keep myself active. I am going to make a pot of tea. She went into the kitchen "Eddie" she called out. Come here.

Young man, Talean was calling you. You better join her in the kitchen

Eddie got up and walked slowly with unsure steps into the kitchen. "Sit right here" pointing him to a chair by the window. You should not go near those two, they were horrible people with fixed ideas We go into the front room after I made the tea. Eddie looked round the small square kitchen.

CHAPTER 27

▼

It was late in the evening. Eddie looked round the kitchen, lots of things in every corner. The table was full of kitchen articles parked high. The wall shelves no longer have covers. You could see all the items stocked in them. Canned food filled two shelves, plates, plastic containers. You name it a mosaic of kitchen articles.. Some of the shelves seemed to have not been used for years. The kitchen looked out was old fashion. The sink was old and rusty.

As Talean mixed the tea cups she said "I give them their tea and we go to the front room alright? " She took the tea tray and beckoned to Eddie to follow. She put a tea stool near her Uncle. She fixed her Aunts tea. "There you are she said. "Lets go to the front room" she said to Eddie. He followed her to a bigger room, with a brightly colored settee and an arm chair near the window. Eddie looked round as she turn on the bright lights. Lots of family pictures. A large imposing marriage picture was sitting on a visible position. That was when Uncle and Aunt married forty five years ago" she told Eddie as he watched the photo. "But these people were now in their seventies. They looked scrumpy and ailing. My Uncle worked in a coal mine for nearly thirty years"

No wonder he looked so frail. Those were their children. The two girls each got married to a white man; and the boy too got married to a white woman. The youngest of the boys has a black girlfriend. One night, I heard him telling the boy on the phone" Do not trust these black women. They were no good."

Talean turned on the big TV set fixed in a wall unit. They sat together and watch the telly.

Eddie sipped his tea lowly. He burnt his mouth with the first sip and now taking his time to get as little as possible into his mouth They did little talking, concentrating on the telly. Talean had her left hand moving all over Eddie's body, caressing his hands, his body, his hair.

"They were going upstairs into their bedroom" she whispered. She pulled herself away from Eddie; her hands were on her laps. She sat stiff, concentrating on the telly.

The door opened slightly "good night young man. We were going to bed now. See you some other time" Mrs. Wright said.

"Good night Uncle and Aunt."

"Well, we have the sitting room to ourselves. " She got up took the tea cups. I just put them in the sink" she said.

Without saying a word Eddie sat quietly watching the telly. He felt a bit gnaw in his Tommy. He put his left hand on it.

Talean came back quietly. "You alright? She asked. She sat near him; put her left hand on his shoulder. She put her right hand on his Tommy. "You hungry I guess."

He nodded. "Oh, I am sorry she said in a soft voice, caressing his back. There was food in the kitchen. I am going to put it in the microwave. We would eat together." She got up, stretched herself. "I am hungry too, but your presence had suppressed my hunger. We were going to have a good meal. I bet you. She walked through the door, turned round to look at him. She smiled and rubbed her hands together and disappeared behind the door.

Eddie sat motionless, he reclined on the settee threw his head back in a sleeping mod.

Eddie come here a minute" Talean called in a low voice. He remained in the reclined position. She came in quietly and stood by him "were you sleeping?" She asked in a whisper. "Lazy Berger you are. Are you too hungry to sit up" poor man it's my entire fault I should have thought about it. We spent the whole afternoon in that flipping hall without even a drink. I guessed you never had any proper breakfast, and no lunch today. Oh me, stupid woman I am. I have lost the art of looking after a man. I am good at looking after a man though, don't doubt me on that. It sounded silly now doesn't it? If I could not look after you now, what else?" but guess what I definitely knew how to make a man happy, for sure. Honest. Soon there will be smiles all over your face I bet you. Let me go and get the food ready first. You stay right where you are while I get the food. I won't be long alright?"

She came back with a plate full of brown rice and peace, two roasted chicken legs and two spoons on a tray.

Eddie had a good look at the plate. The rice had been colored brown by the juice from the beans. Tiny bits of salt fish and cold slaw. "It smelt good. My saliva was already at work" he said still in the reclined position.

"I would spoon feed you if you were too tired to sit up and eat. She sat down, put the tray on her lap, this was your spoon and this is mine. That drink was yours, but you and I would drink from any of the cups. Would that be alright for you?" She took half a spoon full and put it on his lips. He opened his mouth as she pushed the spoon between his lips.

"It tasted real good he sat up, took the spoon and began to eat. She took the flesh from the chicken leg and put it before him. He looked at her, smiled and continued eating. "Why all these, he thought. She pushed her left leg between his and began to grease her leg on his. She looked at him and then he stopped eating for a while, smiled and went on eating again. She had stopped eating, took a spoonful and put it in his mouth. She took the glass of orange juice, drank some, and gave him some to drink; he opened his mouth and took a gulp.

Eddie put the spoon down and fell back on the settee. He closed his eyes briefly. "You had enough?" She asked.

"Yea man" he replied as he felt his Tommy with his right hand. She caressed his Tommy as well, by running her right hand over it, then up his chest. She knuckled his left breast, and then ran her hand slowly down to his belly and then his laps. He straightened his head, looked at her. Her eyes were wide open, burning brightly with tingles of passion flame. He ran his hand over her breast, then dug into her left breast; Knuckled it a few times. A heat wave ran down his spine. She could feel the hot blood running up her body as well. She then put her right leg over Eddie's left thigh. He pulled her over, enclosed her into his arms. They were both in wild kissing mod. His hands were running down her blouse, and into the skirt which was all ready loose. He was exploring every inch of her body and they were both in the dream world of romance" Lets get on the carpet" she told him.

It was Christmas eve. Eddie had moved accommodation twice. He was expelled from the International House at Oakfield road for breaking the rule of not bring a woman into the hostel and not drinking alcohol inside the hostel regarded as a Christian home. It was an international hostel but only African students were accepted into it because they could be treated like children and they would not complain. They had very little experience or none at all on making their voices heard and they feared and respected white people as their colonial masters' These African still had the mentality that white people were superior and black Africans were inferior and so they would accept any condition or regulation from a white person, since their main concern was their education they came to get.

From the hostel Eddie moved into the Griffin Close, a University student campus. He shared a flat with three Kenyan students. Talean had moved in with him at the displeasure of the other students. It was now eight months since they have been together. The course work was over. He and Talean passed the course work.

He was now completing his thesis, which he needed to present to graduate.

Talean had to change two buses to get to work at the day center. Eddie was now a regular visitor at the day center, doing most of the administrative work. If he was not at college, he spent the day at the center, and they both travel home in the evening.

It was one Friday afternoon; Eddie came from the university in time for dinner at the day center. "Hi Eddie" said Faye who stood at the main entrance. "I have a letter that I want you to type for me today. I hoped you don't mind. She was smiling. Eddie stopped to embrace the kid who ran to met him as he entered the hall. "Oh not at all I would do anything for you." he said to Faye. He then took the three year old held her high in the air and then put her down. "She liked you" Faye told him. "May be you looked like her dad, or her mum was your girl friend. Kids do recognize faces, you know. If she had seen you once before, she would always remember you. I guess you have been to her house. Eddie twisted his face. "Do not tell me fips, you know."

"Oh no, far from that I don't even know how her mum looked like. I do not know my way round the city, you know. I only knew how to get here. I have missed the bus stop twice on my way to this place.

You must be stupid then, if you could not remember a bus stop which you used regularly.

It was at the beginning actually while I was still filling my way round. I had problems trying to figure out some land marks close to the bus stop. I now know that the Pump Tavern was next to the bus stop. I would never again miss that bus stop.

I don't believe in that statement, you know" she told him, as she warn off the little boy who came and held her hand, inviting her to play with him.

"Why would you not believe my explanations?" he asked.

"Somebody was going to clip your ear soon."

"Who me, you must be joking. " That would never happen." He shook his head left to right.

"Here she comes" said Faye; as she backed off one step Eddie turn round.

You were here already? I thought you were going to the University first. I thought it was necessary to go there."

I did all I had to do. The rest will wait

The little girl freed herself from Eddie, went and sat on the mat. The children were having their indoor free play. Jen stood by the window watch the kids play.

"I see you later" said Faye, as she moved away. She sat on a chair opposite the entrance. One child came sat on her feet. She rocked the child, keeping an eye on the two by the foyer. She tried to listen to their conversation. "I have some work for you in the office. You want to come up and start shifting through the files.

978-0-595-48486-7
0-595-48486-7